Contemporary Piano Method
book 2A

by Margaret Brandman

Exclusive distributors for Australia and New Zealand
Encore Music Distributors
227 Napier St, Fitzroy VIC 3065 Australia
Phone +61 3 9415 6677
Facsimile +61 3 9415 6655
Email sales@encoremusic.com.au

This book © Copyright 2015 by Margaret Brandman trading as Jazzem Music
46 Gerrale St, Cronulla NSW 2230 Australia
ISBN 978-0-949683-25-0
ORDER NUMBER MMP 8024
International copyright secured (APRA/AMCOS). All rights reserved.

Unauthorised reproduction of any part of this publication by any means,
including photocopying, is an infringement of copyright.

CONTEMPORARY PIANO METHOD - BOOK 2A

INTRODUCTION

This method is designed to equip the student with the necessary skills to play both Classical and Modern music, including Popular and Jazz styles, with ease and understanding while giving experience in skills required for both classical and contemporary examination syllabi. The piano method is the central core of an integrated course which provides materials for ear-training (audio and workbooks), theory, technique, improvisation and repertoire pieces in all styles.

The methodology incorporates various learning styles or modalities, including:

* aural training
* spatial reasoning -visual, aural and tactile
* colour - to impart the meanings of the durations of the notes
* visualisation and the use of pictorial representations of the intervals
* the gestalt approach to topics (the whole view)
* knowledge of keyboard geography
* shape and pattern reading
* harmonic analysis
* improvisation
* transposition

Following on from Books 1A and 1B in the series, this next book continues to feature:

The streamlined interval approach to reading
This is achieved when the aural, tactile and visual aspects of music are combined so that students are able to read and play by following the flow of intervals. Level Two develops the *music speed-reading and learning skills* to a high degree. by encouraging performers to view sections as larger recognisable musical shapes and patterns, including those which span an octave.

Transposition
By combining the interval reading approach with *scale pattern thinking*, students are able to transpose music to other keys with ease. The added benefit of this skill is the security that is instilled in the performer for reading music in the written position in the more advanced keys.

Easy ways to conceptualise rhythm and rhythm notation
The use of diagrams to be coloured in and clapped, helps students to quickly associate a concrete meaning to the language of music rhythm notation and establish a body feel for timing. The use of colour, spatial concepts and the tactile information transferred by the act of colouring, brings into play many accelerated learning concepts.

Keyboard Geography
Continuing from Books 1A and 1B, the *keyboard pattern approach* is used to teach all major and all minor scales in all forms. Students are required to close eyes and visualise their hands on the keyboard pattern for the key before playing the scale and reading the music. Refer to the pictorial patterns for Major scales on page 102 of this book and to the supporting publication *Pictorial Patterns for Keyboard Scales and Chords* for all the *minor* scale patterns.

Understanding Harmonic Structure

A unique feature of this course is that it requires students to be actively engaged in the task of discovering the underlying harmonic structure of music, using the information to speed up the learning process, build an aural awareness of keys and chords, and to use as a basis for improvisation.

Adding to the knowledge of Primary Chords in major keys, gained in Level One, Books 2A and 2B, cover **all** minor keys and chords, and the chords found on the scale degrees in both major and minor keys. (for instance: diminished & augmented chords) The harmonic pallette is further extended to include all the standard four-note chords found in classical and modern pieces.

Improvisation

The knowledge of the *sounds* of scales and chords and their corresponding keyboard patterns is fostered so that they can be used as tools for improvisation. Throughout this book the student will be learning the familiar sound of the **I - vi -ii - V- I** chord progression as used in songs and for use as a vehicle for improvisation.

Books 2B, 3 and 4 of this series build upon the information in this book and move on to cover more advanced Classical, Jazz and Contemporary techniques and the harmonic understanding required for those levels. Topics include: popular dance rhythms, unusual scales, extended and altered chords, modern writing techniques, reading in C Clef, Figured Harmony at the keyboard, Polyphony and many other related topics.

For more detailed information on the ideas and information in the series refer to my web site:

www.margaretbrandman.com

Margaret Brandman (Dr)
Ph.D (Mus/Arts), B.Mus.(Comp), T.Mus.A
F.Comp. ASMC., F.Mus.Ed.ASMC., L.Perf. ASMC
Hon.FNMSM., A.Mus.A., ASA T.Dip.

INTEGRATED SUPPORT MATERIALS FOR THIS LEVEL

* Contemporary Theory Workbook -Book 2
* Contemporary Chord Workbook -Book 1
* Contemporary Aural Course - Sets 2 -4
* It's Easy to Improvise
* Dreamweaving -5 piano solos featuring modern chords
* Blues and Boogie Woogie -12 original solo pieces in swing rhythm
* Twelve Timely Pieces - piano solos in varying time signatures from 2/4 to 7/4
* Christmas Favourites
* Contemporary Modal Pieces - a graded series of pieces exploring modes and 20th century writing techniques

For more detail, refer to page 103

CONTEMPORARY PIANO METHOD
BOOK TWO
CONTENTS PART A

Musical Styles Through the Ages	8
Reading Music	9
Interval Review	10
Review Exercises	11
Counting and Colouring Review	12
Major Scale Review. Cycle of Fifths	14
No. 1 A Little Joke, Brandman. (Mezzo Staccato)	15
Tetrads (Four-Note Chords)	16
No. 2 Russian Folk Song, Beethoven. Primary Triad Review	17
Minor Scales **A Minor**	18
Handy Manuscript Page	20
E Minor Scale New Position Changing Methods Number One Interval Climbers (Fifths)	21
Minor Chords **A and E Minor**	22
No. 3 Winter Waltz, Brandman. How to find the Key	23
Minor Chords in the Major Scale and Major Chord Table. **Phrasing**	24
No. 4 Serenade, Haydn	25
Passing and Auxiliary Notes Music Speed Reading: Interval Climbers (Sixths)	26
No. 5 Jerry's Jump, Brandman (D.C. al Fine)	27
B, D and G Minor Scales and Chords	28
Music Speed Reading: Sixth and Seventh Chord Shapes	30
No. 6 Signs of the Times, Brandman (Dal Segno and Coda)	31
No. 7 Scaling Mount Neverest, Brandman (8va and Loco)	32-33
Naming Intervals	34
Music Speed Reading: Interval Climbers (Sevenths). Accents	36
No. 8 Spanish Accent, Brandman	37
Diminished and Augmented Chords	38
Double Sharp and Double Flat Signs The Complete Major Chord Table. Interval Climbers (Octaves)	39
C and F Minor Scales and Chords	40
No. 9 Rockin' the Beat Along, Brandman	41
Left Hand Accompaniments	42
No. 10 Songbird, Brandman	43
The Minor Chord Table	44
No. 11 Night Flying, Brandman	45
Music Speed Reading: Root Position Tetrad Shapes and Octave Spans	46
Reading Intervals across the Great Staff. The Metronome (M.M.)	47
No. 12 Walkin' Easy, Brandman. Arpeggiando Sign	48
No. 13 Hava Nagila, arr. Brandman	50-51
Dominant Seventh Chords (F, C, G, D, A)	52
Ornaments. No. 14 Grasshopper Hop, Brandman. Acciaccatura	54
Pedalling	56
Pedalling Exercises	57
Chord and Pedal Study in D Major. Appoggiatura	58

No. 15 Falling Leaves, Brandman. Appoggiatura	59
Music Speed Reading: New Position Changing Methods Number Two Chord Climbing using Root Position Triads	60
No. 16 Old Dance Tune, Purcell	61
Chord Naming Systems No. 1 **Figured Bass**	62
Chord Naming Systems No. 2 **Modern Chord Symbols**	63
Music Speed Reading: Chord Climbing Exercises, First Inversion Triads	64
Wraggle Taggle Gypsies, O! When Johnny Comes Marching Home: Arranging	65
The Sound of Intervals	66
Music Speed Reading: Chord Climbing Exercises, Second Inversion Triads	67
Suspended Fourth Chords	68
Ostinato Bass	69
Trill. Repeat Bars	70
No. 17 The Rumble, Brandman	71
Position Changing	72
New Position Changing Methods No. 2 Helping Hand Exercises	73
Helping Hands – Left Hand Crossing Right	74
No. 18 Leaping Lizards, Brandman	75
Helping Hands – Right Hand Crossing Left	76
No. 19 Leaping Frogs, Brandman	77
Pedal Point	78
No. 20 Undercurrents, Brandman. Mordent	79
Jazz Timing. Boogie Woogie Left-Hand Patterns	80
The Blues Scale and Blues Notes	81
Improvising over a twelve-bar blues using a Boogie pattern and the Blues scale	82
F sharp and C sharp, Minor Scales and Chords	83
F and C Minor Contrary Motion Scales	84
No. 21 Go for Baroque, Brandman. Inverted Mordent	85
Music Speed Reading: Tetrad Shapes. Root, First and Second Inversion Shapes	86
No. 22 Minuet in G, Bach	87
Chord Progressions based on the Cycle of Fifths	88
Improvising on a chord pattern	89
New Position Changing Methods, Number Three. Shifting Shapes over the Interval of a Third	90
Shuffle Rhythm Patterns for Two Hands. Improvising Practice	91
No. 23 Sans Souci Shuffle, Brandman	92-93
Cadences	94
Playing Cadences	95-96
No. 24 Boogie Shake, Brandman. Tremolo	97
Diminished Seventh Chords	98
Chord Pattern	99
No. 25 On the Upturn, Brandman. Turn	100
Pictorial Patterns for Major Scales	102
Integrated Support Materials	103
Handy Manuscript Page	104

CONTEMPORARY PIANO METHOD
BOOK TWO
CONTENTS PART B

Modulation	111
No. 26 Gavotte, Handel	113
No. 27 Turn It Down, Brandman. Inverted Turn	115
Principles of Fingering	116
Tierce de Picardie	119
No. 28 Bateau Blue, Brandman. Speed Markings	120
Chords used for changes of sound colour	121
No. 29 Waltz for Kirk, Brandman. Swing Waltz	122
No. 30 Grecian Dance, Brandman. 7/4	123
B flat, E flat and A flat Minor scales and chords	124
Major Seventh Chords	126
Scale and Chord summary	127
No. 31 Sarabande, Handel	128
Chord Pattern using Major Sevenths. Suggested Practice Routine	129
Melodic Minor Scales. **A, E and B Minors**	130
Major Sixth and Minor Seventh Chords	131
Cycle progression	132
Rock Chord Pattern, Brandman, using Major Sixth chords	133
Country and Western playing style Major Scales over Two Octaves	134
No. 32 Roumanian Ride, Brandman. 7/8	135
D and G Melodic Minor Scales	137
Popular Dance Music of the Twentieth Century	138
The Tango, Brandman. Glissando	139
No. 33 Tango Azul, Brandman	140
Part Playing	141
C and F Melodic Minor Scales	143
No. 34 Sarabande, Buxtehude	144
Rock Chord Pattern using Major Sixths and Minor Sevenths	145
B flat, E flat and A flat Melodic Minor Scales	146
No. 35 Chacabuco, Cha Cha Cha Brandman.	147-148

Minor Sixth and Minor Seventh Flattened Fifth
   (Half-Diminished Seventh) Chords 149
No. 36 Jucaro Rumba, Brandman 150-152
F sharp and C sharp Melodic Minor Scales 153
Cycle of Fifths 154
The Bossa Nova 155
No. 37 Bossa Nova de Bondi, Brandman 156
Improvising on a chord pattern 159
Swingin' in Style – chord pattern, Brandman 160
No. 38 Al's Café, Bailey 161-164
No. 39 Blueberry Ballad, Brandman 165
No. 40 Beneath the Coolabah Tree, Brandman 166
Crotchet Triplets 167
Crotchet Triplets continued and the Duplet 168
No. 41 Spiderswing, Brandman 169-172
Rhythmic Chord Patterns:
    Conga 173
    Motown 174
No. 42 Jingle Bells - disco/reggae arrangement, Brandman 175-176
No. 43 Benny's Beguine, Brandman 177
Rhythmic Chord Patterns: Jazz-Rock, Funk and Disco Patterns 179
No. 44 Funky Dancin', Brandman 181
Simple and Compound Intervals 184
No. 45 Sydney Samba, Brandman 186
No. 46 Make Mine Mambo, Brandman 189
No. 47 I'll Never Break Your Heart, Wilde and Manno – Popular Sheet Music 191
Advanced Modulation Spider Chart for Major Keys 196
Advanced Modulation Spider Chart for Minor Keys 197
Signs and Terms used in this Book 198
Suggested Practice Routine 199
Integrated Support Materials 200

MUSICAL STYLES THROUGH THE AGES

Throughout the centuries there have been certain distinct styles, each of which was current for a number of years, much as popular music goes through phases, each one of which is distinguished by a few notable performers and composers.

In the Western musical tradition (Europe, England, America and Australia) the first evidence of this was available with the advent of written music which was initiated by the Monks in the thirteenth century. It is from the written music that the Music History books take the general characteristics of the period and formulate a name for the period.

It must be borne in mind however, that there is a largely unwritten folk tradition in all countries which has always existed alongside the written music of the time. Many composers in all periods have drawn on this folk tradition for melodic inspiration.

The main musical periods and some of the important composers for each period are outlined below.

1. Ars Antigua   c1200-c1325   Adam de la Hale
2. Ars Nova   c1300-c1450   Guillaume de Machaut
3. Renaissance   c1450-c1600   Dufay, Josquin des Pres, Tallis, Palestrina, Lassus, Gibbons.
4. Baroque   c1600-c1750   Monteverdi, Lully, Purcell, Scarlatti (A) Bach, Handel, Buxtehude.
5. Rococo   c1750-c1770   Couperin, C.P.E. Bach, Stamitz.
6. Classic   c1770-c1830   Haydn, Mozart, Beethoven (early style).
7. Romantic   c1830-c1900   Beethoven, Schubert, Schumann, Brahms, Liszt, Chopin, Wagner, Grieg.
8. Impressionist   c1870-c1910   (French Style, concurrent with German Romantics), Debussy, Poulenc, Ravel, Satie.
9. Late Romantic   c1900   Tschaikovsky, Mahler, Elgar, Holst, Saint Saens, etc.
10. Modern (a) Serial c1920. Schoenberg, Alban Berg, Krenek, Stravinsky.
    (b) Neo-Classic c1920. Hindemith, Bartok, Prokofiev, Stravinsky.
    (c) Electronic from 1914 onwards. Russolo, Varese, Schaffer, Schillinger, Krenek.
    (d) Microtonal. R.H. Stein, Bloch, J.H. Foulds.
    (e) Jazz c1900 on. Refer to a volume on the history of Jazz as there are too many personalities to make a selection from.
    (f) National Styles. Australian, American, Canadian, Japanese, etc.

There is not space in this Volume to give a detailed explanation of each period. However, it is suggested that the student refer to a reliable History of Music edition to seek out the background to the music set out in this book.

Any knowledge gained is an aid to the appreciation of the style and sound of the piece.

READING MUSIC

In Book One of the Contemporary Piano Method, playing the keyboard and reading music by intervals (distances) was approached from the point of view of the "Five Finger Hand Position".

With this position, five fingers are set over five consecutive notes and all intervals up to an octave take their bearings from this position, the octave being the largest distance most hands can reach comfortably. (Some people can stretch further but the octave is still a comfortable distance to stretch).

In this book, the "Octave Hand-Span" will be the point of reference for many interval exercises and pieces and the other smaller intervals will be felt in relation to this octave span.

Fingering

The system of fingering used in this method, is based on the concept of the "Key" fingering, that is, one fingering number which suggests a new hand position. For instance, it is considered redundant to write the numbers 1, 2, 3, 4, 5 over notes which are moving in stepwise fashion.

A special feature is that when fingers are to be changed on a held note, the fingering will often be shortened to a dash followed by the change-over finger. For example: "−2" (which implies to 2) instead of "1-2", or "−4" instead of "5-4".

This system presumes that the player will complete the previous section on the correct finger and assumes that the important feature to concentrate the attention on is the **change-over** to the new position.

A Suggestion for Teachers
concerning the encouragement of
IMPROVISATION

Apart from the chord based styles of improvisation covered in Books One and Two of this series, other forms of Free Improvisation can be introduced at an early stage if the teacher so desires, provided that the teacher himself is familiar with the suggestions for Improvisation given in Book 3 of the series. If it is felt that the student is able to cope with and comprehend the more unusual scale sounds, these provide excellent vehicles for guided improvisation in less structured situations. Many very descriptive pieces can be improvised using the techniques suggested in Book 3 of the series.

A note of caution, however: do not introduce the material before the student has grasped the basics, otherwise the amount of material may confuse and dismay the student, and destroy his/her concept of the appropriate styles for particular situations.

INTERVAL REVIEW

In Book 1, the Intervals (distances) of a Unison (same notes), Step (2nd), Skip (3rd), Skip-plus-one (4th) and Jump (5th) were first introduced. Added to these were the 6th, 7th and 8ve (Octave).

REVIEW EXERCISES

1. Here are some review exercises on intervals up to a Jump or 5th.
   Once the position is set, listen to what you are playing and do **not look at your fingers.**

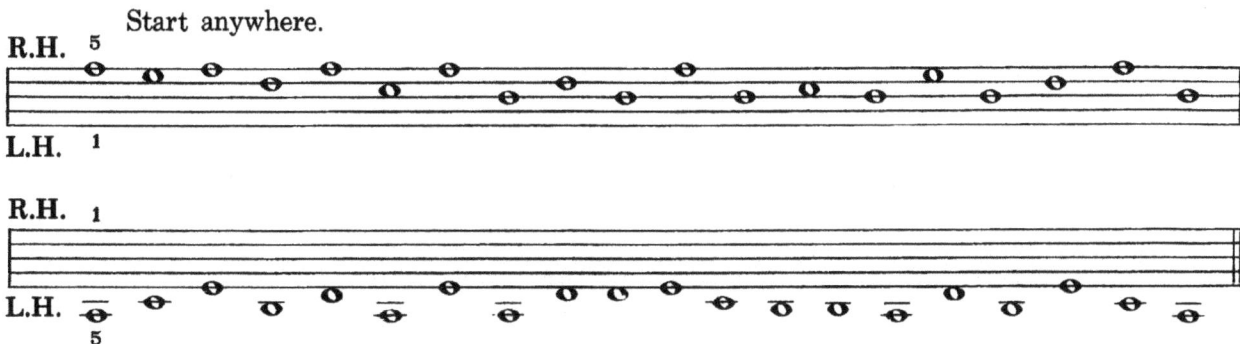

2. Review exercises on intervals up to an Octave.
   Play the following lines either on white notes or on the Major scale patterns that you know.

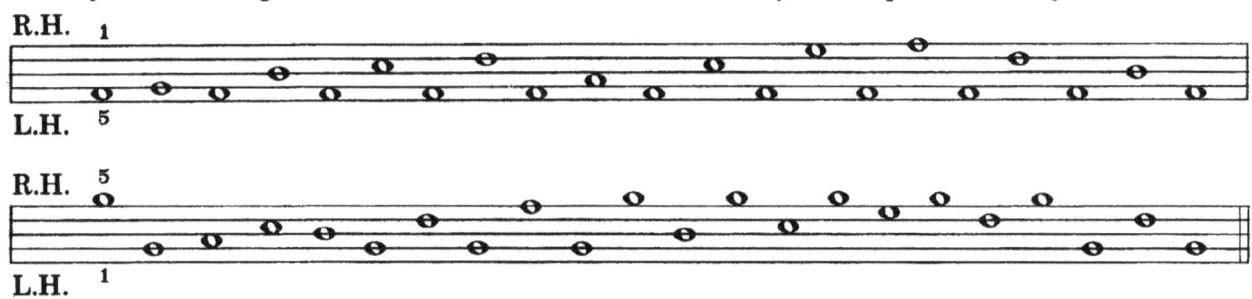

3. Review exercises using all intervals up to an Octave and position changes.

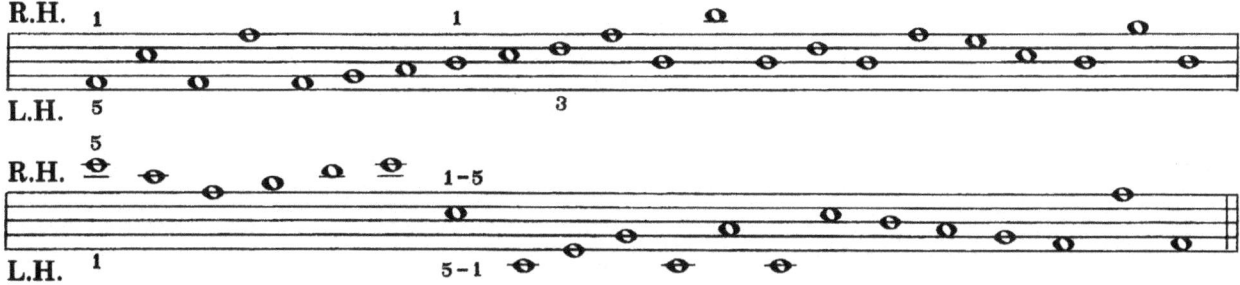

4. Review exercises using Accidentals.

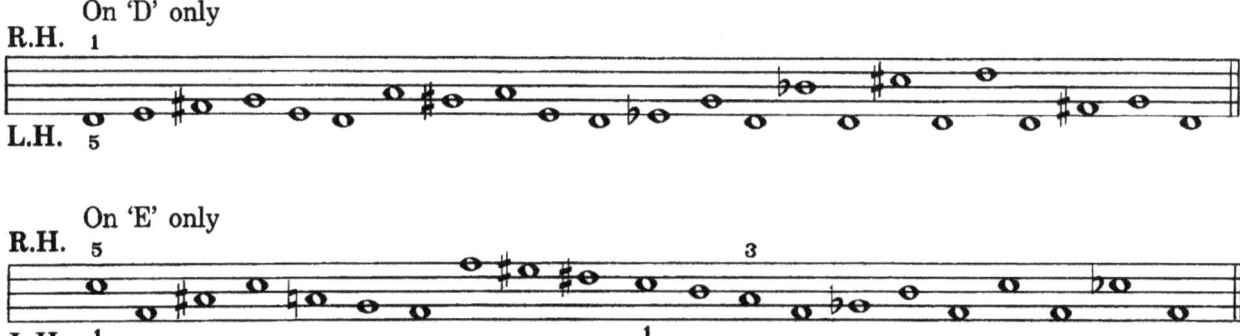

COUNTING AND COLOURING REVIEW

Following the same system used in Book 1, colour in the boxes below the notes. Continue the colour for the length of the note. If there are two notes of the same value placed next to each other, use the contrasting colour of the set, (i.e. dark blue followed by light blue). Do not colour in the boxes representing **rests.** For ties and dotted notes, continue the one colour for the extra length required.

Once the boxes are coloured in, clap the timing while counting out aloud and then play the exercises.

COLOUR SETS:

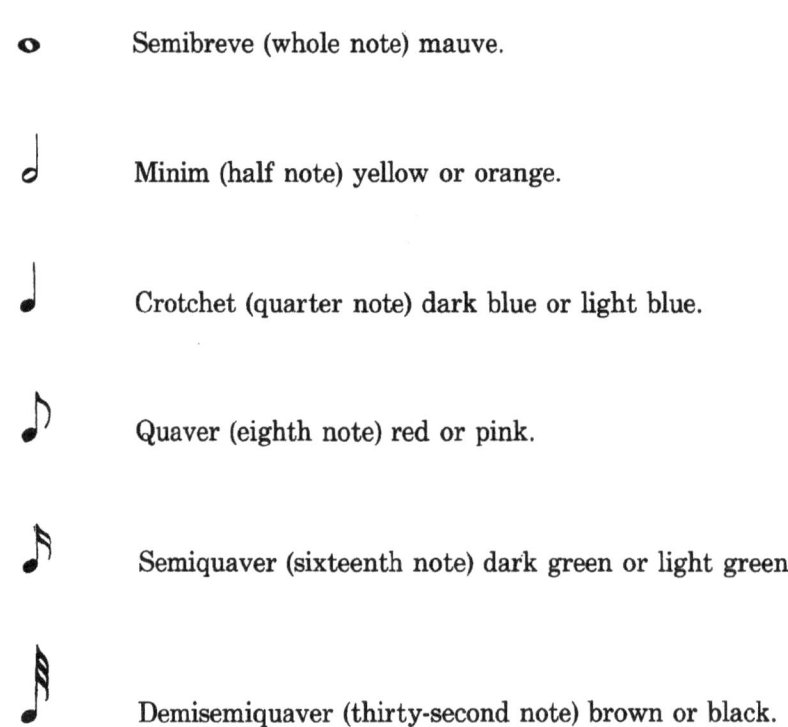

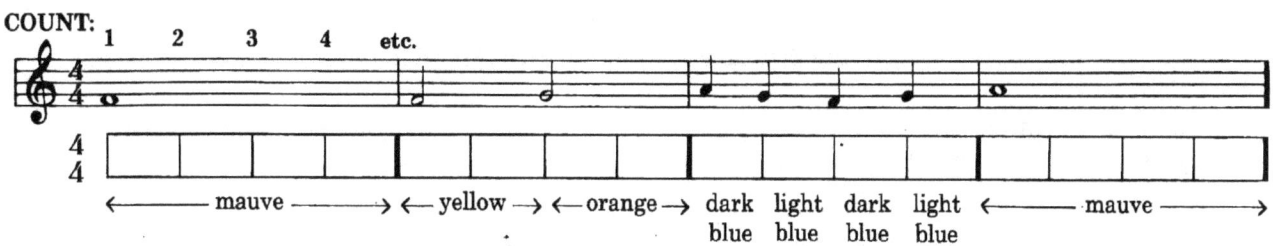

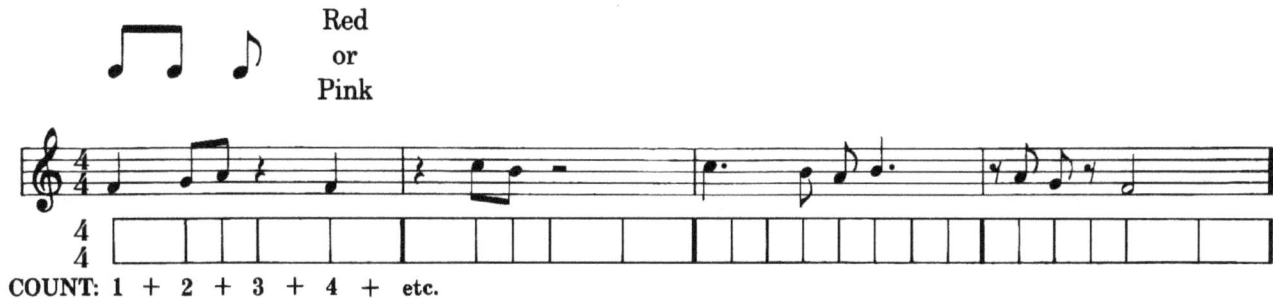

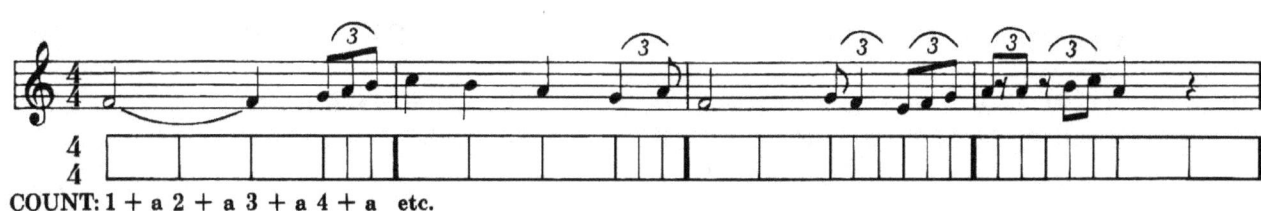

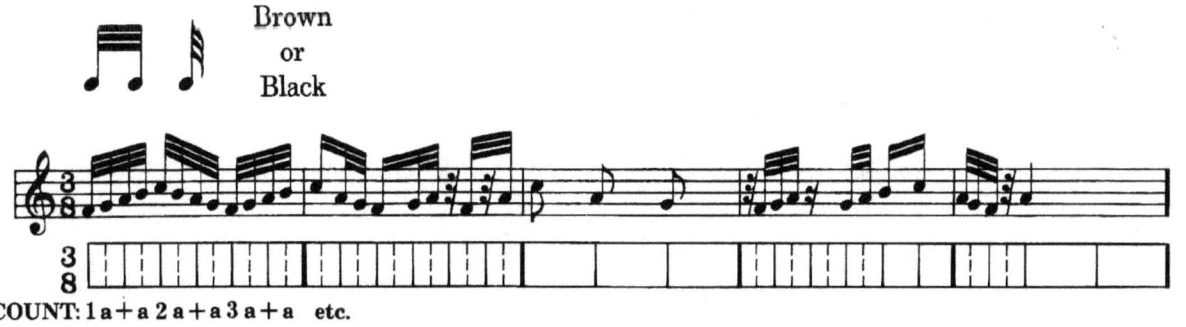

SCALE REVIEW

Before moving on in this Book, you will need to know thoroughly all 12 Major scales over one octave and all 12 Major Chords and Keys as presented in Book 1.

You will also need to know the Primary Chords in each Major Key. (Refer to page 40 in Book 1).

Below is a **summary** of all the **fingering** for the Major Scales and chords, and a diagram of the **cycle of fifths** which shows the key relationships and the number of sharps and flats for each scale.

SUMMARY of SCALE FINGERING

		Left Hand	Right Hand
Group 1.	C G D A E.	5 4 3 2 1 3 2 1	1 2 3 1 2 3 4 5
Group 2.	B	4 3 2 1 4 3 2 1	Same as Group 1
	F	Same as Group 1	1 2 3 4 1 2 3 4
Group 3.	B flat	3 2 1 4 3 2 1 3	4 1 2 3 1 2 3 4
	E flat	" " " " " " " "	3 1 2 3 4 1 2 3
	A flat	" " " " " " " "	3 4 1 2 3 1 2 3
	D flat	" " " " " " " "	2 3 1 2 3 4 1 2
Group 4.	F sharp	4 3 2 1 3 2 1 3	2 3 4 1 2 3 1 2

N.B.

Right Hand **Fourth** Finger on B flat (A sharp) in all scales in which the 4 is printed in heavy type.

TRIAD FINGERING

	Root Pos.	1st Inv.	2nd Inv.	Root Pos.
Right Hand	135	125	135	135
Left Hand	531	531	521	531

CYCLE OF FIFTHS

ORDER OF FLATS   **ORDER OF SHARPS**

B♭ E♭ A♭ D♭ G♭ C♭ F♭   F♯ C♯ G♯ D♯ A♯ E♯ B♯

FLATS ←——————   C   ——————→ SHARPS
                         0
              F   G
              1   1

          B♭ 2   2 D

          E♭ 3   3 A

          A♭ 4   4 E

              D♭ 5   5 B
                    6   6
                    G♭   F♯

In this Book these scales will be used as the basis from which the Relative Minor scales are found.

MEZZO STACCATO (HALF STACCATO)

The strict interpretation of a staccato dot is that it shortens the note by half the written value. Usually, however, it is simply played short and crisp, the exact length being dependent on the speed and style of music and the performer's taste.

If the strict interpretation of the staccato dot were to be followed then the Half or Mezzo Staccato marking would mean that the note would be shortened by a quarter of its value. Depending once again on the style of music, the Mezzo Staccato can be played anywhere between a quarter and a half shorter than the written value of the note. In other words not as short as a staccato note would be in the same piece of music.

FOR EXAMPLE (a) Full Crotchet
                  (b) Mezzo Staccato
                  (c) Staccato

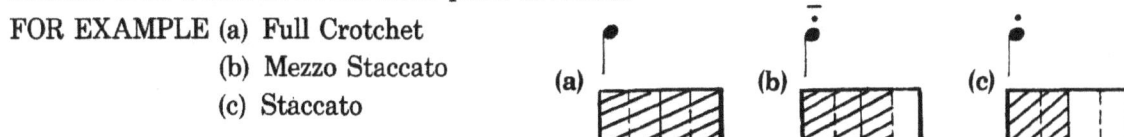

1. A LITTLE JOKE

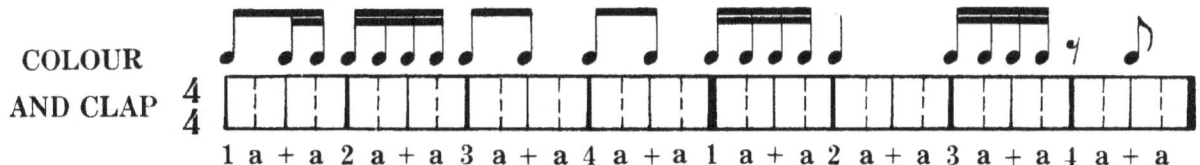

Subito — abbreviation "sub" — suddenly.

Scherzando — playfully

TETRADS

Tetrads are four-note chords which span the octave. (From the Greek word 'tetra' meaning four) The basic three-note construction has an added octave from the lowest note.

The general principle involved in the fingering of these chords is to use the first and fifth fingers to span the octave and to use the fingers which fall comfortably on the other notes in-between.

Play all Major and Minor tetrads and their inversions, first in block form until secure and then in broken form.

The Right Hand fingering shown on these examples is the same for each of the chords, while the Left Hand fingering for the Root Position tetrads of D, A, E, B and F sharp major is: 5 3 2 1

BLOCK FORM

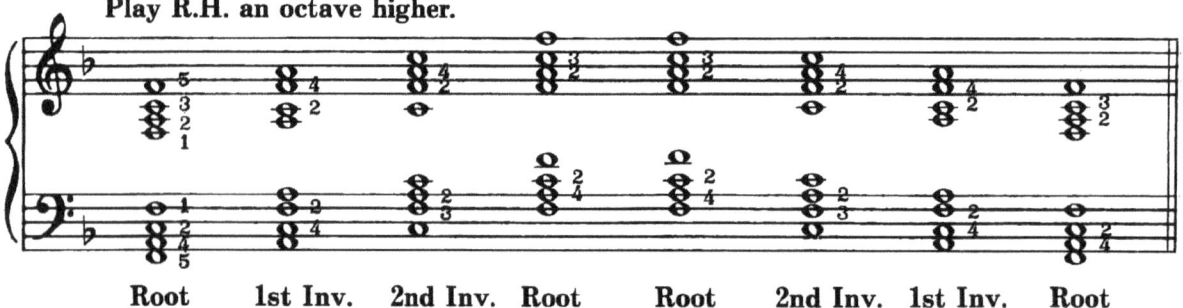

BROKEN CHORD FORM

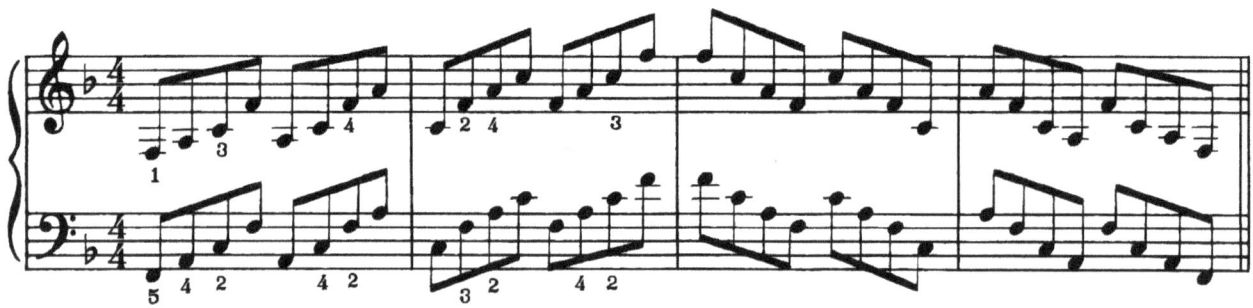

N.B. Those students with small hands need play only the Broken form of the four-note chords.

PRIMARY TRIAD REVIEW

The Primary (most important) Triads built on the notes of the Major Scale are the Tonic Triad (I), the Dominant Triad (V) and the Subdominant Triad (IV).

They can be arranged into a Table of Chords in this manner — IV, I, V –, so that they can be seen as part of the Cycle of Fifths. In a Major Scale these chords are always Major Chords.

2. RUSSIAN FOLK SONG

Complete the Table of Primary Chords for the key (scale) of this piece. Try to find these chords in the music and then write the chord names above each bar.

COLOUR AND CLAP

COUNT: 1 a + a 2 a + a 1 a + a 2 a + a 1 a + a 2 a + a 1 a + a 2 a + a

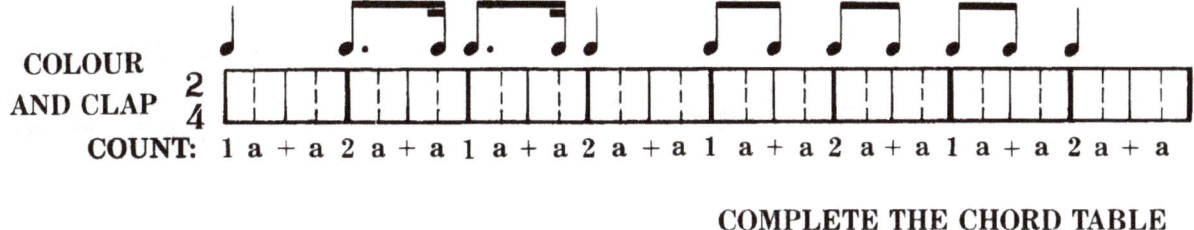

This piece is in BINARY form. It has **two** contrasting sections. These can be marked as sections "A" and "B".

COMPLETE THE CHORD TABLE

IV	I	V

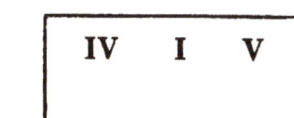

* *Phrasing — see page 24.*

Ludwig Van Beethoven, 1770–1827
German, Classical and Romantic style

Vivace — Lively

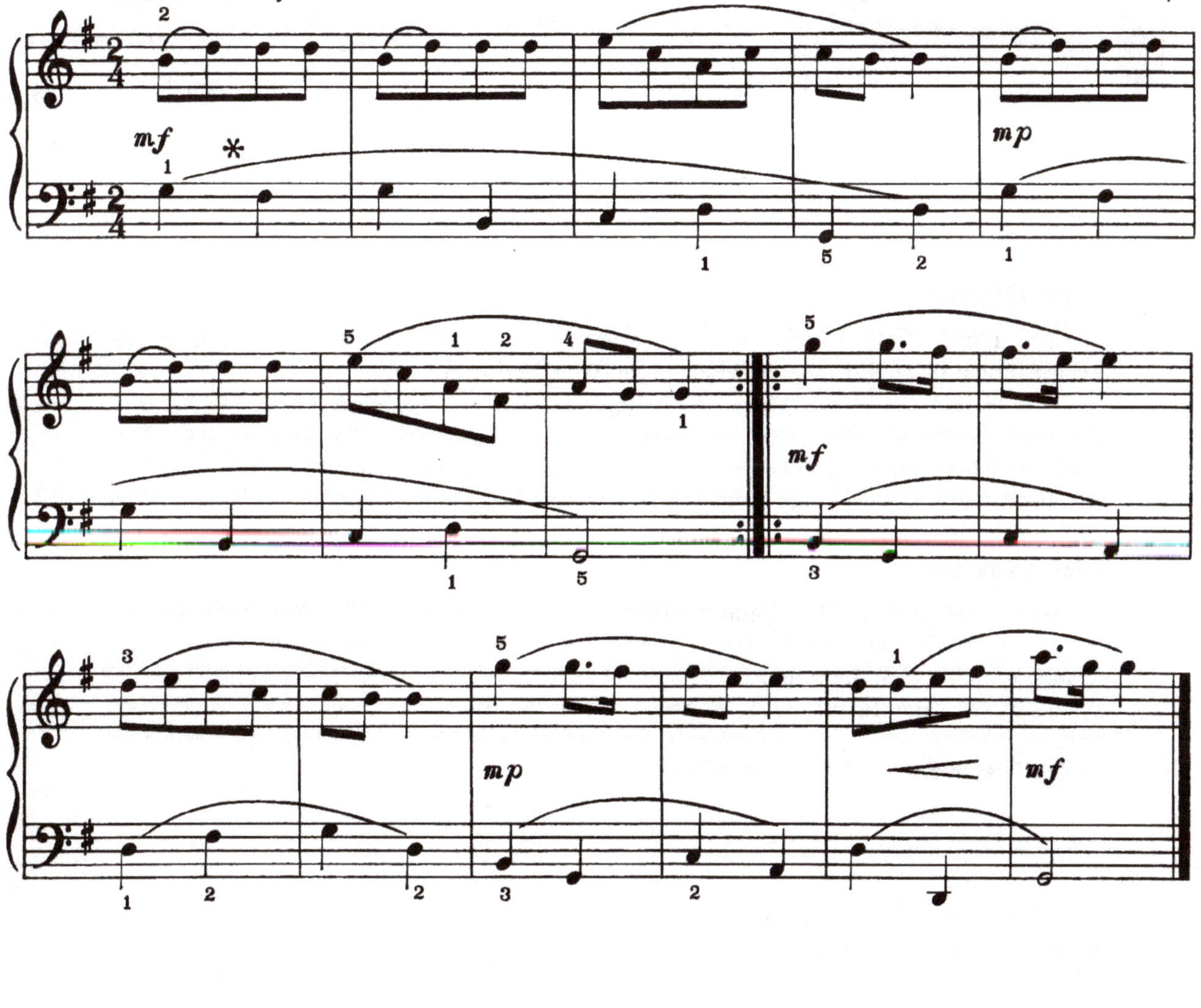

MINOR SCALES

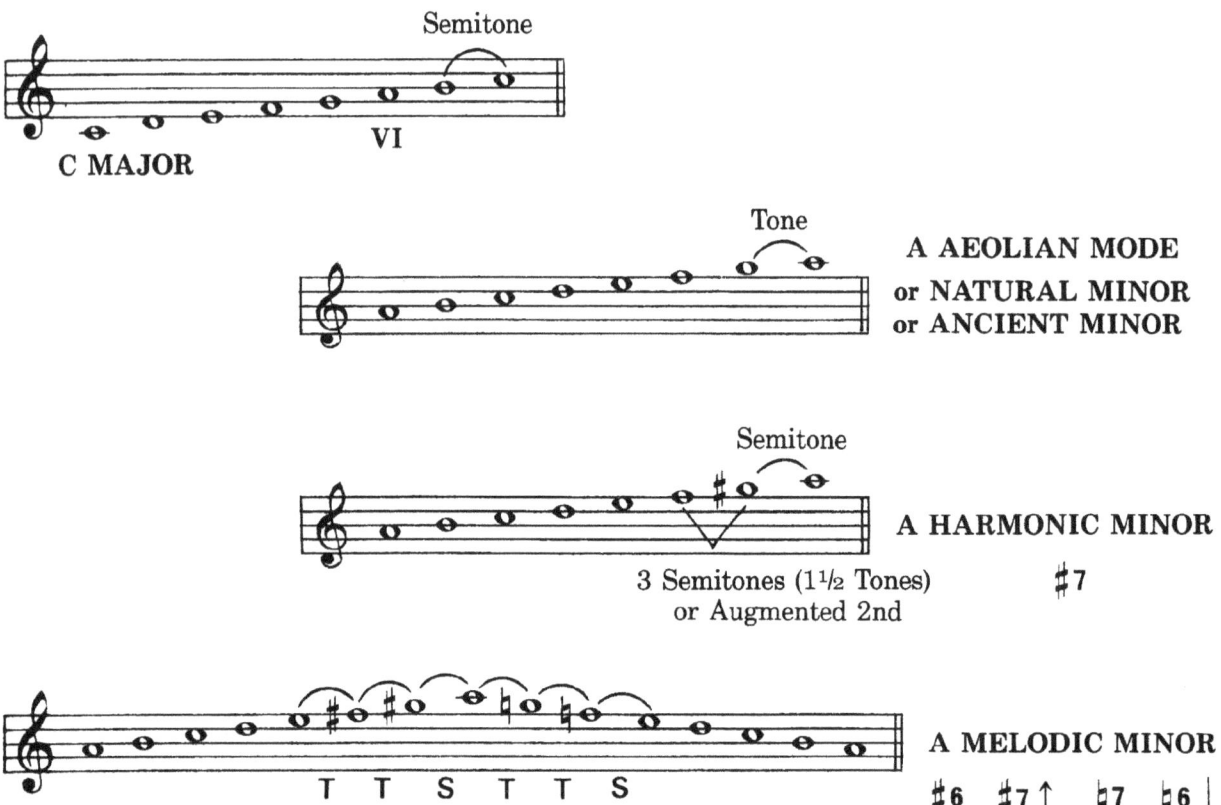

THE MODES

The major scale which has been discussed in Book 1 has its origin in the Ecclesiastical or church Modes which date from Medieval times.

It is in fact the Ionian Mode which happens to be all the white notes from C to C. The other Modes are also found on the white notes of the piano. For instance from D to D on the white notes is the Dorian Mode. The Aeolian Mode is the scale from A to A on the white notes and it is this Mode which has now become the foundation for the Minor Scales used in Western Music.

RELATIVES

As C major (Ionian Mode) and A minor (Aeolian Mode) are both white notes scales it is easy to see that they both have the same Key Signature and are therefore related or *Relative* scales. C is the Relative Major to A Minor and vice versa. (Just as brothers and sisters of the same family have the same last name, Smith or Jones). As A is the sixth note of C major scale, one can see that the **Relative Minor is found on the sixth note of the Major Scale.** (See the example).

To fully understand to topic of Minor Scales and Minor Keys students are advised to complete lessons 5 -11 of *Contemporary Theory Workbook* - Book 2 (Brandman).

NATURAL MINOR

The Aeolian Mode is commonly known today as the *Natural Minor*, or Ancient Minor. In other words, the scale with the same key signature as its relative major with no alterations. Always play this form of the minor scale before moving on to the other forms of the minor shown in the example.

HARMONIC MINOR

To alter the Natural Minor to the Harmonic Minor Form, the **seventh** note must be raised. If you compare the major scale to the natural minor you will find that the distance between the 7th and 8th notes is a *Semitone* in the major scale whereas in the natural minor the distance is a *Tone*. Play the two scales and note that the major scale seems to finish more strongly than the natural minor. By raising the seventh note the distance between the 7th and 8th degrees in the harmonic minor matches that of the major and provides a strong finish to the scale. Also when the **chords** are built on the scale notes, the Dominant Chord becomes a major chord and provides a strong resolution from dominant (V) to tonic (I). The word Harmony refers to the chords, hence the name *Harmonic Minor*.

MELODIC MINOR

However, a third form of the scale is needed for **melodies.** When the 7th is raised in the harmonic minor an awkward interval is created between the 6th and 7th notes of the scale. This interval is an augmented 2nd. Try singing the harmonic minor and you will see the effect of this. To "smooth out the bumps", the sixth note is also raised so that the intervals become a tone (5-6), tone (6-7) and a semitone (7-8), and the scale still finishes strongly. However, in the descending form of the scale the strong finish is not required so the other combination of tones and semitones can be used. The 7th and 6th are lowered or in the case of A minor, Naturalised. The distance then becomes tone (8-7), tone (7-6) and semitone (6-5). This form of the minor is therefore called the *Melodic Minor*. Note also that the descending form of this scale is exactly the same as the *Natural Minor*.

In this book all the Harmonic Minor Scales are presented in sequence, then the same is done with the Melodic Minors. I believe that it is easier to learn all the scales of one type first and understand the basic Key Signatures. When these are understood, learning the Melodic form is no problem.

As each Harmonic Minor Scale is learnt, play it over one octave ascending and descending in the form given below. Note that the Harmonic Minor form of the scale uses the same notes both ascending and descending.

The fingering for **A minor scale** is the same as for **A Major Scale.**

A HARMONIC MINOR

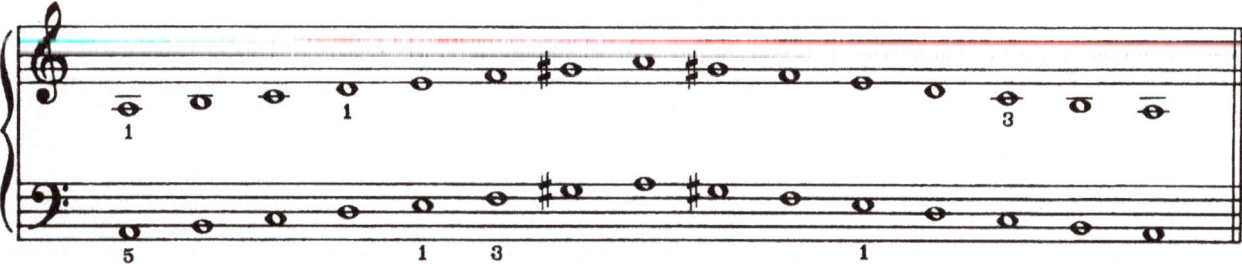

Refer to the keyboard patterns for the three forms of the minor scales in all keys on pages 17-34 of *Pictorial Patterns for Keyboard Scales and Chords* (Brandman).

HANDY MANUSCRIPT PAGE

Music Speed-Reading
New Position changing methods - Interval Climbers

This is the first of the new methods of changing position to be learned in this book. In an interval climbing exercise, the hand is required to shift position by a step for each pair of notes. In this case for each interval of a 5th (jump).

Practise these reading exercises separate hands first and then hands together. Start on any note you choose, except an F or A.

INTERVAL CLIMBERS

No. 1 FIFTHS

E MINOR SCALE

E minor scale is found on the sixth note of G major scale and therefore has the same key signature, one sharp (F♯). The Harmonic Form has D sharp as the raised 7th. Both A minor and E minor have the same fingering as C major scale. Play and listen to these scales.

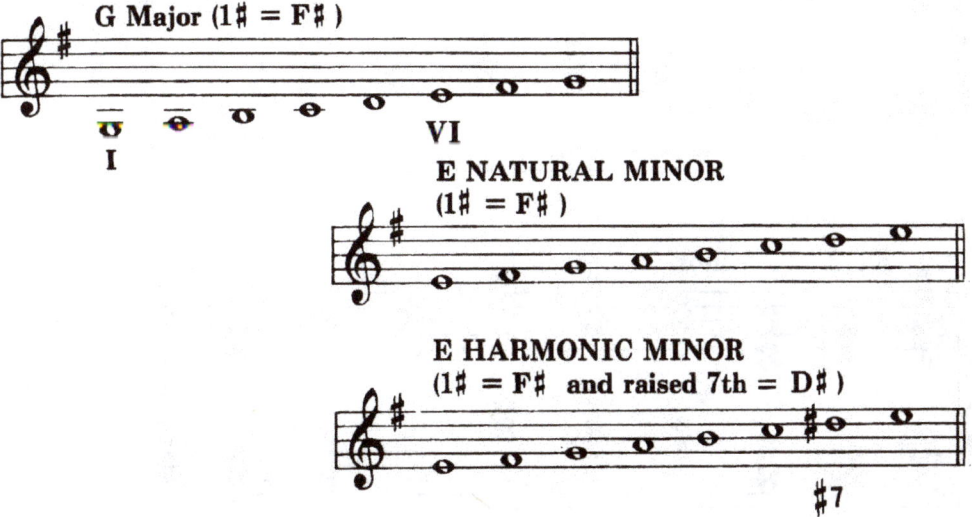

A AND E MINOR CHORDS

The chords or triads built on the tonic notes of these scales are minor chords.

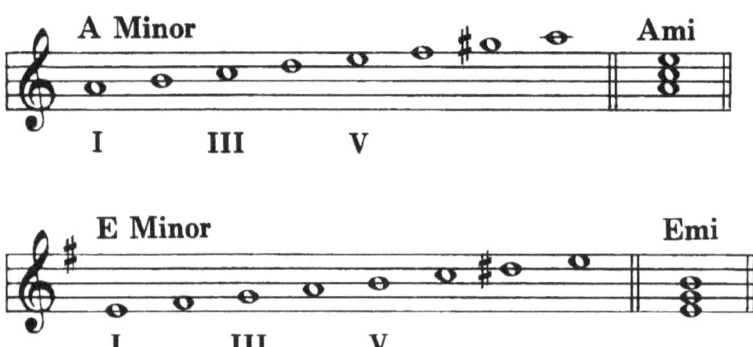

Notice the difference in sound between a major and a minor chord. The major sounds quite bright whereas the minor sounds a little sad. Note the intervals between the chord notes. In the major chord there is a distance of 4 semitones between the tonic and the mediant notes and 3 semitones from the mediant to the dominant note. In the minor it is the reverse — 3 semitones from I to III and 4 semitones from III to V.

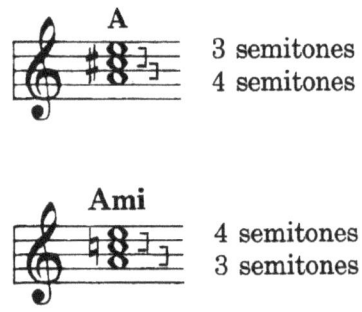

Play A and E Minor Triads in Root Position and inversions in Block and Broken chord styles. Learn the three-note chords and inversions first then practise them as four-note chords and inversions. See examples 1 and 2.

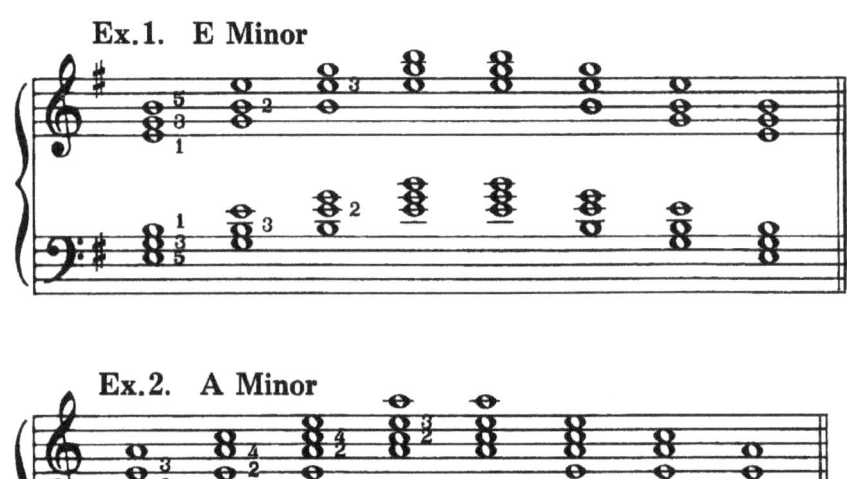

WHAT KEY IS THIS PIECE IN?

When working out the Key (scale) of the piece you are playing there are several clues to look for:
1. Look at the Key Signature (i.e. the number of sharps or flats at the beginning of the line).
2. You now know that any Key Signature could mean either the Major Scale or its **Relative Minor**. To decide which, look at the final chord in the piece and particularly the lowest note in the Bass part, (the **root** note of the chord). This final chord will be the Tonic chord (Chord I) of the key.
3. If you think the scale is in the Relative Minor, look through the body of the piece to find accidentals indicating the Raised Seventh note of the Minor Scale.

3. WINTER WALTZ

COLOUR AND CLAP

KEY: ....

THE TABLE OF CHORDS

At this stage the table of chords can be extended to include the minor chords which occur on the 2nd, 3rd and 6th notes of the Major scale.

They are known as Secondary Chords whereas the chords on I, IV and V are the Primary chords. (The chord that occurs on the seventh degree is introduced on page 38).

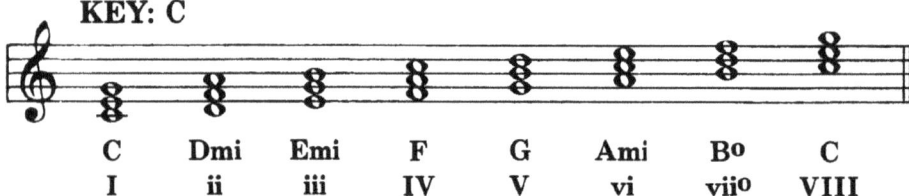

Place the secondary chords under the Primary chords in this manner so that the Relative Minors are under the major chords.

IV	I	V
F	C	G
ii	vi	iii
Dmi	Ami	Emi

Write this table anywhere you have space alongside the piece you are playing. When you compare the chords above and below one another you will find there is only one note difference between the two. Therefore, quite often one can be substituted for the other. Music that uses the minor chords is more harmonically interesting from that which uses only the Primary triads. You will probably find more of the minor (secondary) triads the further you progress.

PHRASING

The short slur marks between two notes and the longer phrase marks over sections of music indicate that notes should be joined together smoothly and that the finger should be lifted off the note at the end of the marking.

Slurs add aural colour and interest to music, as do phrase markings. Phrase markings in particular can be thought of as "breath" marks. If you were singing the line, the logical place to breathe would be where the phrase ends. If you think of phrases this way, it is easy to provide your own phrasing to a piece without phrase markings. (For instance, much of J. S. Bach's music is published without phrase markings or with editorial markings that you may not agree with).

Phrase marks help to shape the music and enhance the melodic line. Play the piece given opposite with and without the markings and note the difference to the shape and sound of the melody.

4. MAIN THEME OF THE SERENADE

(from String Quartet Opus 3, No. 5)

COMPLETE THE CHORD TABLE

IV	I	V
ii	vi	iii

Andante = **at an easy walking pace.**
Cantabile = **in a singing style.**

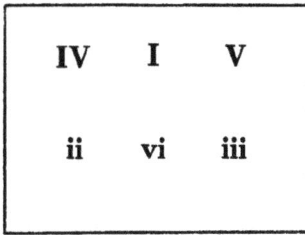

COLOUR AND CLAP

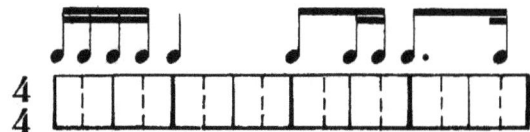

Study Procedure.
First write in the chord names.
Next block out the chords or five finger segments.
Finally, play as written. Think of the Left Hand notes as Bottom, Middle or Top notes of the chord.

Joseph Haydn, 1732–1809
Austrian, Classical Style

Andante Cantabile

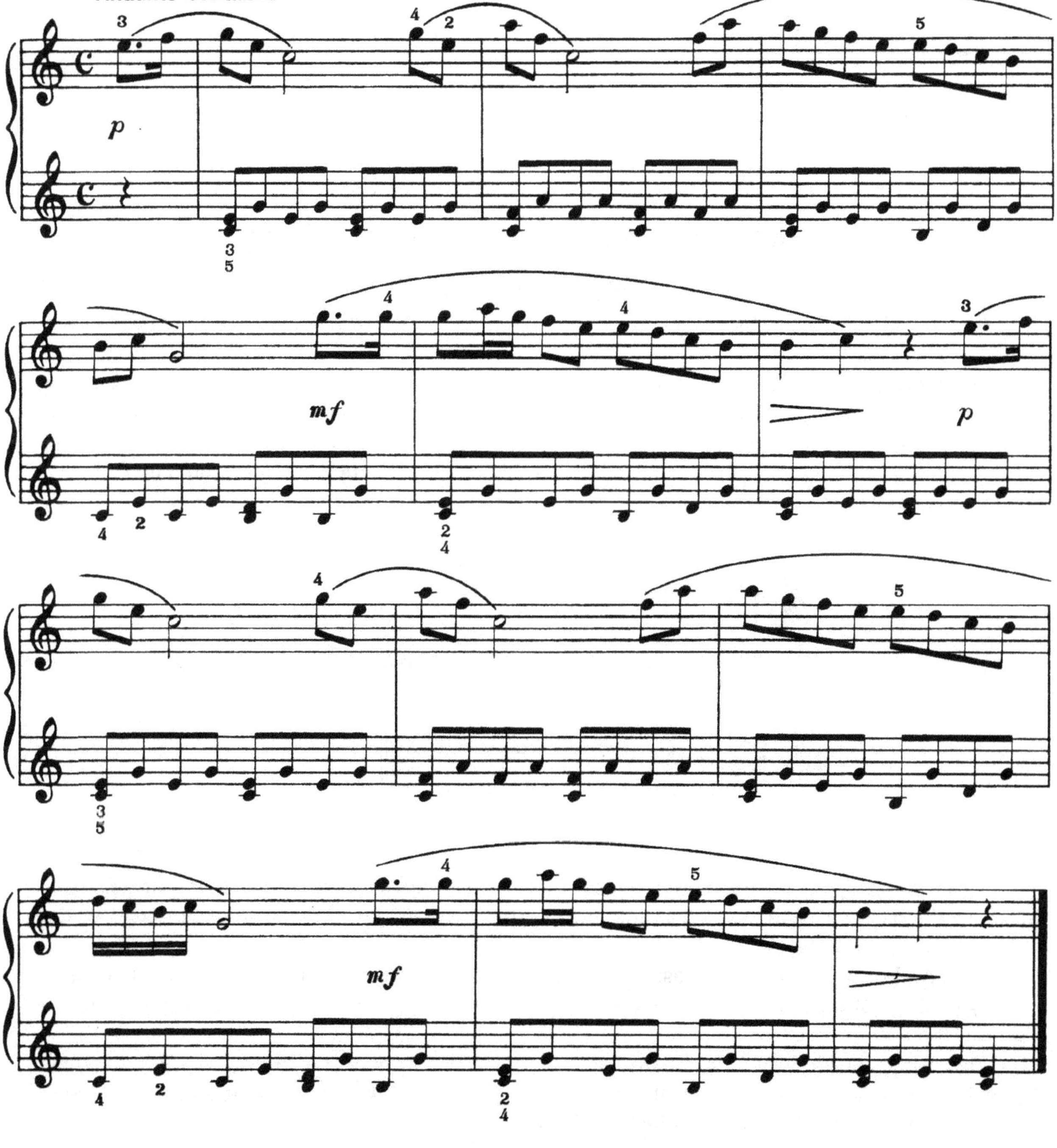

Music Speed-Reading
Interval Climbers - SIXTHS

Play in the same manner as number 1 (page 21). Start on any note except D or B.

No. 2 SIXTHS

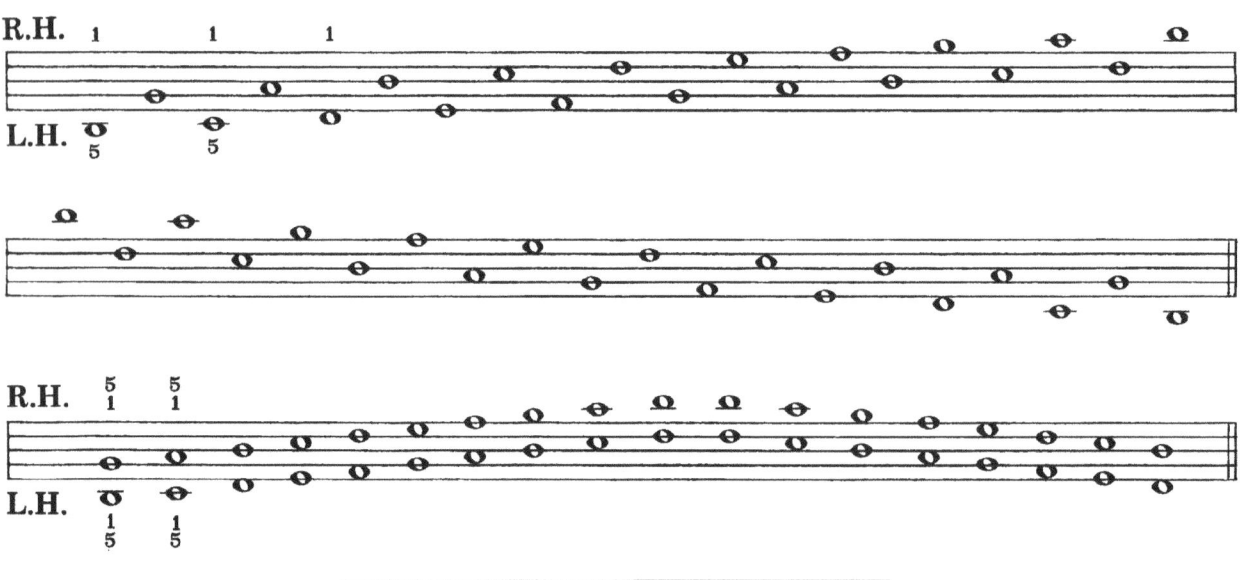

PASSING AND AUXILIARY NOTES

A "Passing Note" is one that fills the gap between two chord notes.

An "Auxiliary Note" is one that moves away from the chord note by step and then comes back to it.

When looking at C Major Triad in relation to C Major scale, we find that the 1st, 3rd, 5th and 8th notes are chord notes, while those in between can be used as either Passing or Auxiliary notes.

For instance, the second note of the scale, "D" could be used as a Passing Note between the 1st and 3rd notes, "C" and "E", OR it could be used as an Auxiliary note moving one step up from "C" or an Auxiliary note moving one step down from "E".

When working out the chords for the pieces that you play, be aware of the fact that not every note in the bar is a chord note. Passing and Auxiliary notes do not have to be included in the chord name for the bar.

Usually, but not always, the Passing and Auxiliary notes will be found on the weaker beats of the bar, (the 2nd beat or 4th beat in 4/4 or on the second quaver in a group of two quavers for instance).

Once again make use of the Chord Table for the piece in question to help you decide which chords are the most likely to occur in that key, and therefore which of the notes you see are chord notes and which are Passing and Auxiliary notes.

The **STACCATISSIMO** sign is a small wedge placed near the note head.
Play the note as short as possible.

Special Note: When the wedge is found on music of the Classical Period it signifies Mezzo-Staccato.

More Repeat Signs: As well as the double dots, the other methods of indicating repeats are by the words **Da Capo al Fine**, usually abbreviated to **D.C. al Fine. Da Capo** means go to the **Head** (or beginning) of the piece. **Al Fine** means play until you see the word **Fine** or simply the end of the music.

5. JERRY'S JUMP

When working out the key remember that the final chord is found at the word FINE.
FINE (pronounced: fee-nay) is the Italian word for conclusion or end.

COMPLETE THE CHORD TABLE

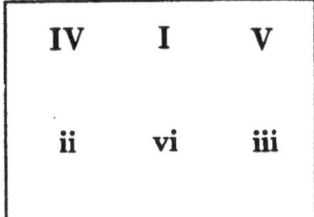

Write in the Chord names above each bar (measure).

Clap through the timing of the notes on the Treble stave before playing this piece.

MINOR SCALES: Bm, Dm, and Gm.

On page 18 the formation of Minor Scales was discussed. Below are three more minor scales that can now be added to your scale programme.

B HARMONIC MINOR SCALE

B Harmonic Minor is related to D Major. (B is the sixth note of D Major Scale). The Key Signature is therefore the same as D Major; i.e. 2 sharps — F sharp and C sharp. Play the Natural Minor scale first, from B to B with F sharp and C sharp and no alterations. Secondly, raise the Seventh note to convert the scale to the Harmonic Minor form. This will mean that you play A sharp instead of A for the Harmonic Minor Scale. Also look at the pattern of black keys as was done for the Major Scales.

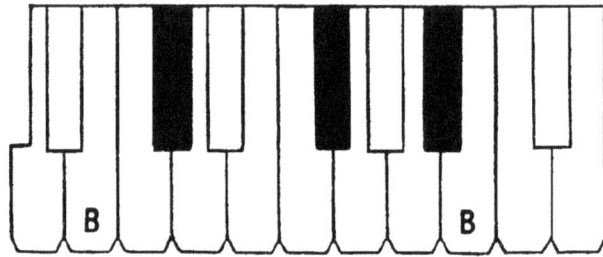

The fingering is the same as B Major — right hand: 1 2 3 1 2 3 4 5 and left hand 4 3 2 1 4 3 2 1.

Try to think of A, E and B minors as a set. If you look at the pattern of black and white notes on the 6th, 7th and 8th notes of the scales you will notice the similarity: white, black, white.

D HARMONIC MINOR SCALE

The next two scales are also a set, if regarded in this light. D minor is related to F major and therefore has one flat, B flat. Play the Natural Minor first, then raise the seventh note from C to C sharp for the Harmonic Form. The 6th, 7th and 8th notes are now black, black, white.

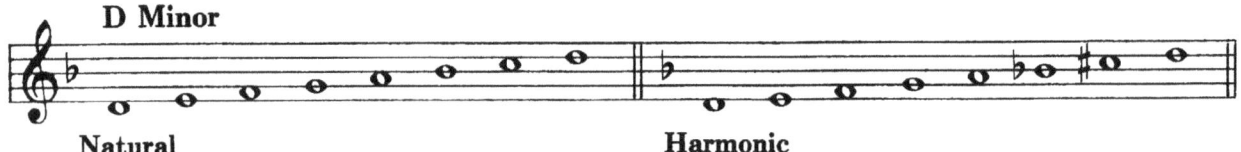

G HARMONIC MINOR SCALE

G Minor scale is related to B Flat Major. (2 flats — B flat and E flat). Play the Natural Minor form first and then raise F to F sharp for the Harmonic form. Notice that the pattern of black and white notes on the 6th, 7th and 8th degrees, is similar to the pattern in D Minor scale.

B, D, AND G MINOR CHORDS

Chords. Work out the minor chords belonging to the above scales, by taking the 1st, 3rd and 5th notes from the scales. You will find that the notes in **B Minor** chord are B, D, F sharp; in **D Minor** chord: D, F, A and in **G Minor** chord: G, B Flat and D.

Play the minor chords you have learnt thus far (G, D, A, E, B) in both Block and Broken form, in inversions, as you have been doing with the Major chords.

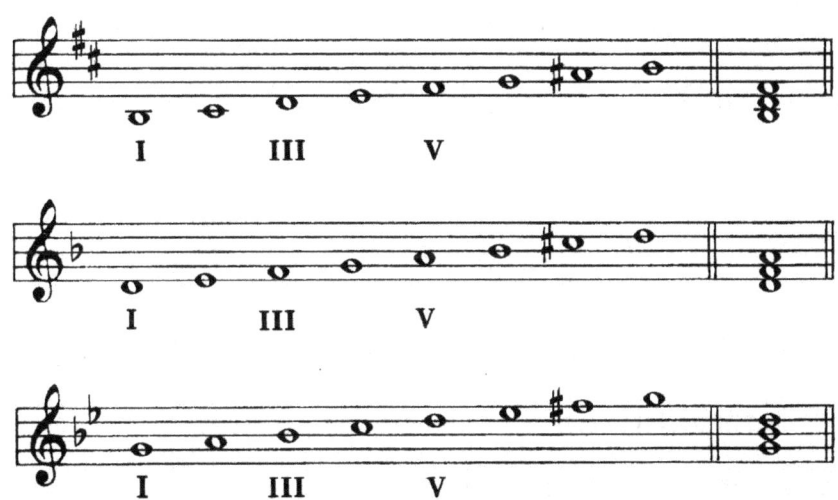

A AND E HARMONIC MINOR   CONTRARY MOTION SCALES

Contrary Motion. At this stage you should begin to play the minors previously learnt (A and E) in Contrary Motion. Remember to play the right hand up and back first, then the left hand down and up and then put them together. Look for patterns, for instance, when the black notes occur at the same time.

THE CHROMATIC SCALES

Do not forget to continue playing the Chromatic Scale. (See Book 1, page 64). At this stage in your study, it could be extended to a two-octave scale starting on any of the twelve notes of the octave.

Music Speed-Reading
Sixth and Seventh chord shapes

Many pieces require the hand to be set over spans of a 6th, 7th or octave. Look along the line of music to see how much of the tune can be handled by one of these positions and set the fingers accordingly.

Once the position has been found, it is useful to think of the four notes as either the Bottom, 2nd, 3rd or Top note of the position, rather than trying to work out each interval individually.

Use this system when playing the exercises given here and on the following pages, and you will find that you can play them much more fluently.

Once again this shows that once the mind has analysed and understood the written figures, the physical execution of the passage becomes an easy matter.

Interval Exercises over the span of a SIXTH

These exercises require the hand to be set over a span of a sixth. As a result, one of the distances of a 3rd (skip) has to be handled by a finger extension or stretch.

Once the position has been found, retain it until the end of a line.

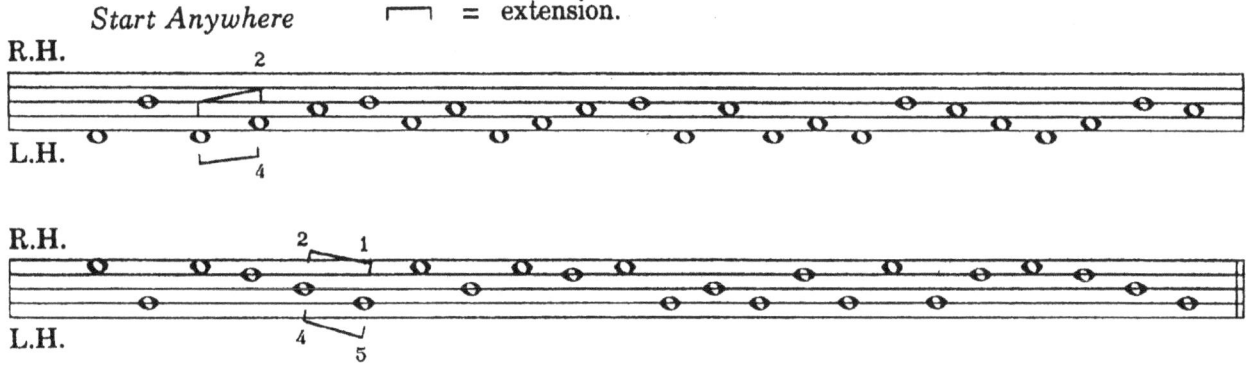

Interval Exercises over the span of a SEVENTH

This set of exercises requires the hands to be set over a span of a seventh. As a result, **two** of the distances of a 3rd (skip) has to be handled by finger extensions. Once again retain the position until the end of the line.

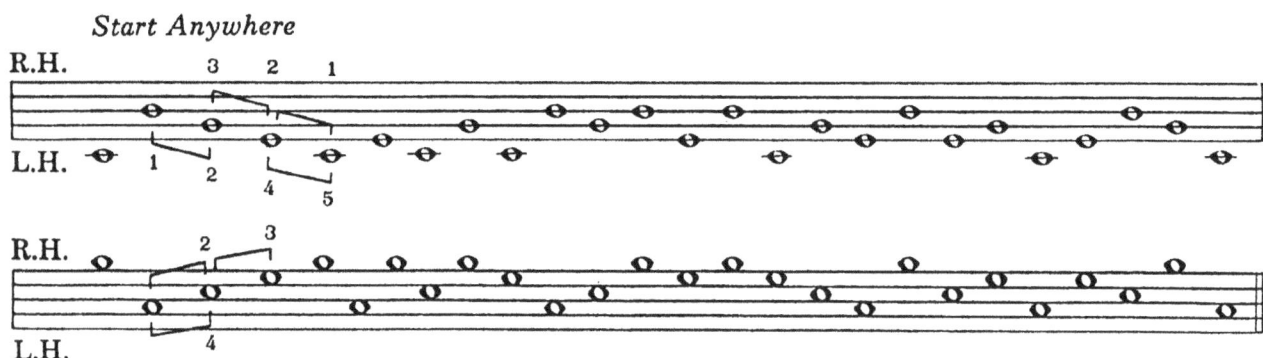

6. SIGNS OF THE TIMES

WRITE CHORD TABLE HERE

Write the Chord names above each bar (measure).

Dal Segno (D.S.) means go back to the sign. 𝄋 (Segno)

Coda literally means "Tail-piece". The sign looks like this: ⊕

   Play the piece through until you come to the Dal Segno, marking (𝄋) then return to the sign (𝄋) at the beginning of the music and on the second playing, jump from the Coda sign (⊕) in the body of the music, to the section at the end marked by another Coda sign. (⊕)

   Also look for **D.C. al Coda** in which case you take the Coda sign after repeating from the **beginning.**

   Clap through the timing of the notes on the Treble stave before playing this piece.

8va (Ottava). If this is placed over the note, play the note one octave (8 notes) higher. Similarly, if it is placed under the note play one octave lower.

LOCO: Play as written.
Latin: "in (the usual) place".
Used after 8va to indicate the return to the written position.

Technique Tip

Prepare for the change of position well in advance.

7. SCALING MOUNT NEVEREST

COMPLETE THE CHORD TABLE

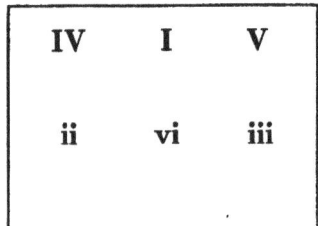

COLOUR AND CLAP

Ghosting the Octave: Move around the instrument using spatial orientation. Find any hidden octaves and use the octave-swap technique to move your hand into the new area or register of the keyboard. (Refer to page 46 in CPM Book 1A)

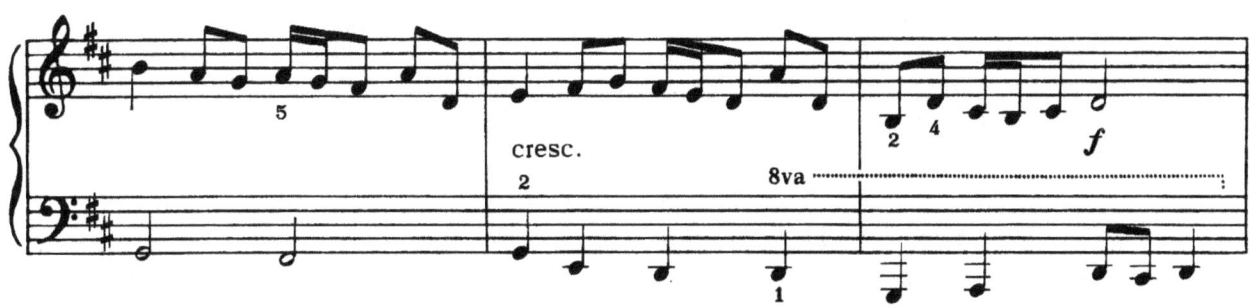
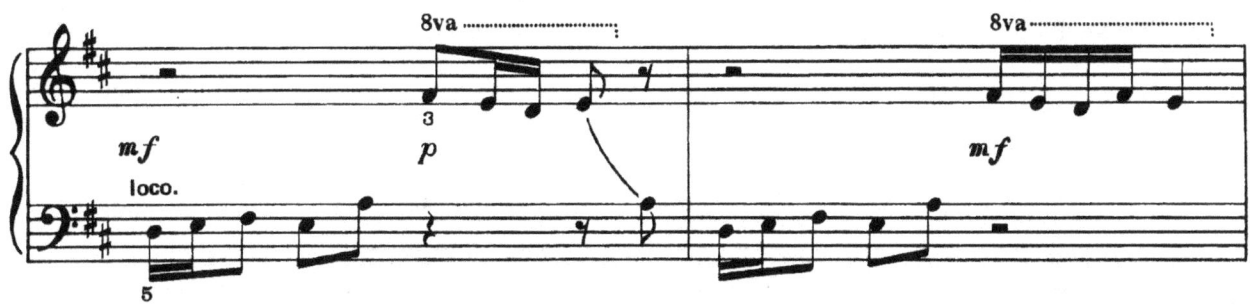

INTERVALS

An Interval is the **distance** between two notes.

The naming of intervals is based on the intervals found in the Major Scale. For instance, the distance from C to D, (in C Major Scale) is a Major Second, from C to E is a Major Third and so on. These intervals are known as Diatonic Intervals or intervals derived from a Diatonic Scale. (A diatonic scale is a scale which uses a mixture of Tones and Semitones, unlike the Chromatic Scale which consists of Semitones only). The Perfect and Major intervals are all found in the Major Scale.

PERFECT INTERVALS — Unison, Fourth, Fifth, Octave

Four of the intervals are known as **Perfect** Intervals, that is, they are acoustically Perfect in sound, smooth with no dissonance. They are found in the Overtone series or Harmonic Series. The first overtone or Harmonic of any note is the Octave above. If you have ever blown across the lip of a soft-drink bottle and then blown harder, you will have noticed this phenomenon. On a Keyboard instrument, the unison and octave are tuned to a precise mathematical proportion, and the Perfect Fourth and Perfect Fifth are as close to Perfect as the modern tempered scale will allow.

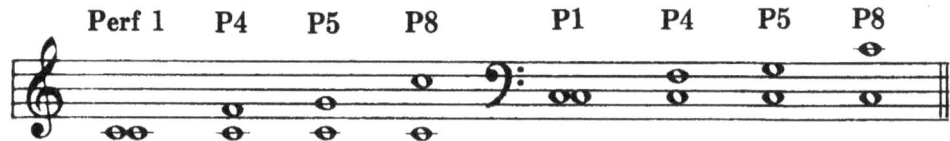

MAJOR AND MINOR INTERVALS

The other intervals in the Major Scale are all "**Major**" intervals, but the word in this case should be taken to mean "**Greater**" intervals. (Major 2nd, 3rd, 6th and 7th).

If these "Greater" intervals are lowered by a semitone they become "**Minor**" or "**Lesser**", intervals. (Minor 2nd, 3rd, 6th and 7th). Thus "Minor" intervals are not necessarily part of the Minor scale, as the terms Major and Minor mean **qualities of scale sounds** when used to describe the scales.

Therefore, when referring to Intervals, always take the Major Intervals from the Major Scale and simply lower them a semitone to find the Minor Intervals.

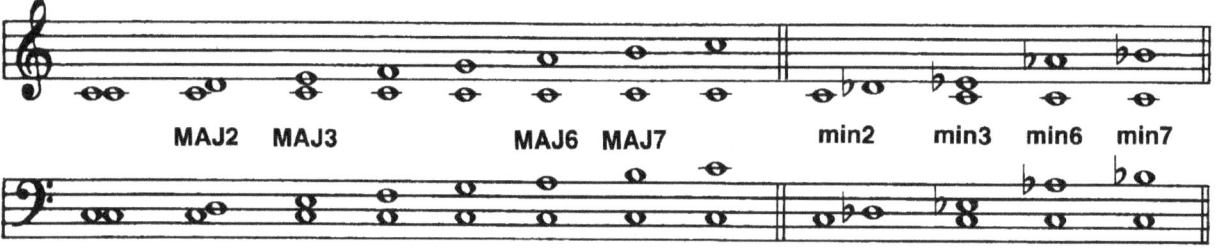

DIMINISHED AND AUGMENTED INTERVALS

When a Perfect Interval is **lowered** by a **semitone** it becomes a **"Diminished"** (smaller) Interval, for example a Diminished Fifth.

When a Perfect Interval is **raised** by a **semitone** it becomes an **"Augmented"** (larger) Interval, for example an Augmented Fourth.

When a Major Interval is lowered the first time it becomes a **Minor** Interval and if **lowered** a **second** time it becomes **Diminished**.

When a Major Interval is **raised** by a **semitone**, it also becomes **Augmented**.

For Example:

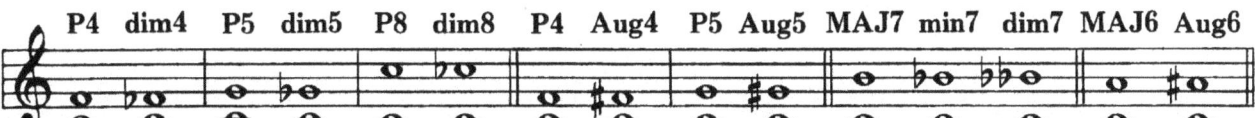

```
Diminished ←── Minor ←── Major ──→ Augmented
Diminished ←─────── P E R F E C T ───────→ Augmented
```

HARMONIC AND MELODIC INTERVALS

Intervals are referred to as **Harmonic** if played simultaneously and **Melodic** if played in succession.

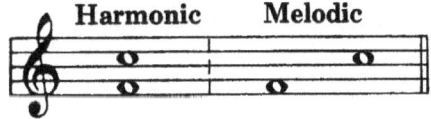

Refer to Contemporary Chord Workbook, Book One.

Music Speed-Reading
Interval Climbers - SEVENTHS

The following exercises on Climbing Sevenths sound pleasant when played hands together beginning an Octave and a Third (Tenth) apart.

Play in the same manner as Numbers 1 and 2. Start on any note except E or G.

No. 3 7ths

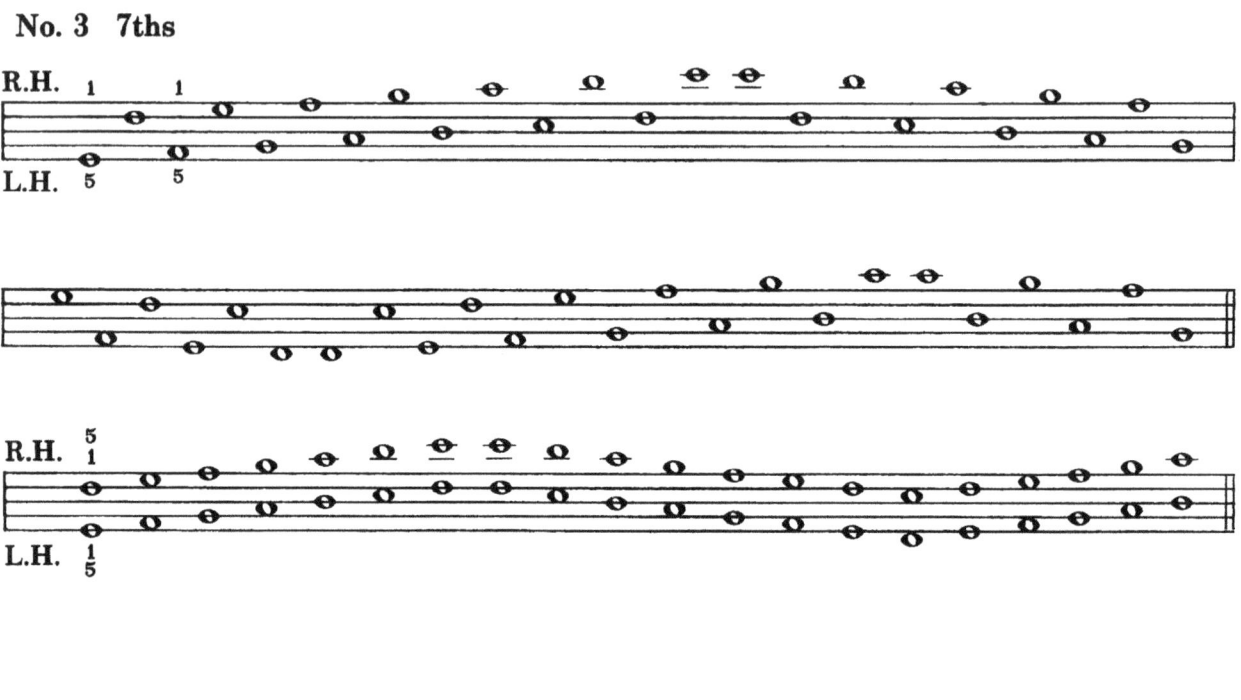

ACCENTS

The following definitions are the accepted interpretations of the Accent signs in popular music, particularly in stage band music (charts). Other variants may occur in Classical music.

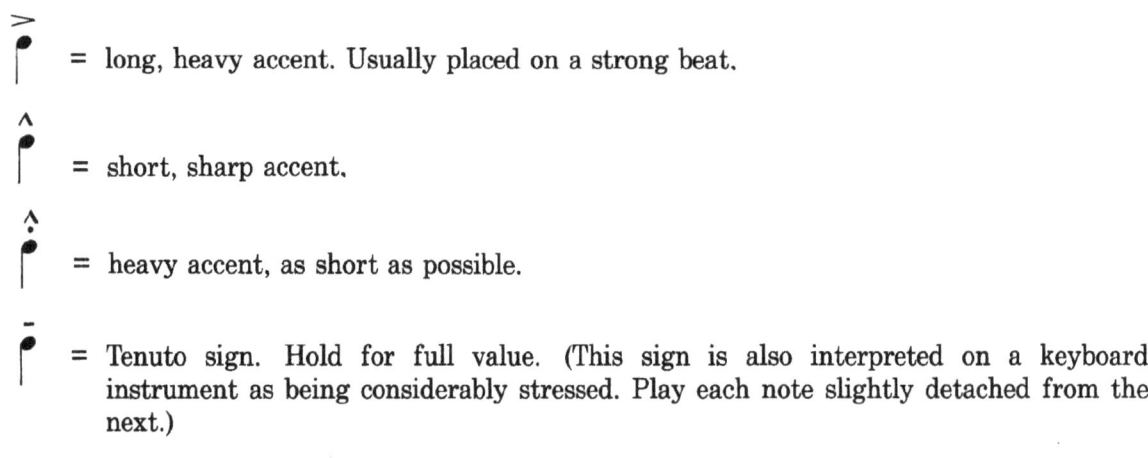

8. SPANISH ACCENT

COLOUR AND CLAP

WRITE CHORD TABLE HERE

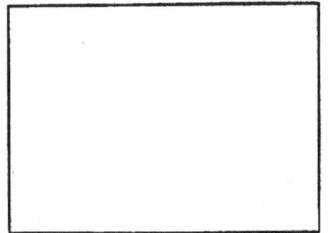

DIMINISHED AND AUGMENTED TRIADS

These two triads must also be known in addition to the Major and Minor triads. The Diminished Triad is found on the seventh note of both the Major and Harmonic Minor Scales and the Augmented Triad occurs on the third degree of the Harmonic Minor Scale.

The word "diminish" means to make smaller. Therefore the Diminished triad is made up of two of the smaller Minor Third intervals (3 semitones), built on top of one another, whereas the Major Triad as seen previously consists of a Major Third (4 semitones) and a Minor third (3 semitones). The other way to work out the Diminished triad is to take a Major triad and lower **both** the **3rd** and **5th** degrees a semitone each.

DIMINISHED TRIAD

The chord functions as a strong leading triad and generally requires resolution onto the Tonic chord of the key.

A leading function triad creates tension which needs to be resolved. Therefore, usually the diminished triad is followed by a Rest Chord. (The Tonic triad, Major or Minor, functions as a Rest Chord).

The symbol for a Diminished triad is a small circle beside the letter name thus: G°.

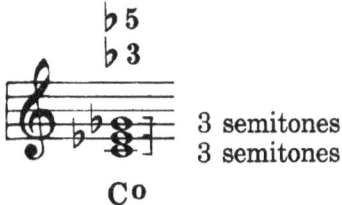

AUGMENTED TRIAD

The word "augment" means to make larger. Therefore, the Augmented triad consists of two of the larger Major Third intervals (4 semitones) built on top of one another. The other way to work out the "Augmented" triad is to take a Major triad and raise the 5th degree a semitone. This chord is most often used as a variation of the Dominant Triad which once again has a strong leading function and resolves onto the tonic triad.

When you work out all the Augmented triads on the twelve keys, you will discover that there are in fact only **four** augmented triads, and the only way to tell them apart is by the way they are written. Due to the symmetricality of the triad, the Augmented triad on C (C, E, G sharp), when placed in the first inversion is the same as the Augmented triad on E (E, G sharp, B sharp or C). Thus if you work out the Augmented triads on the notes C, C sharp, D and E flat and play them in inversions you will have covered them all.

The symbol for an Augmented chord is a small plus sign beside the letter name, thus G+.

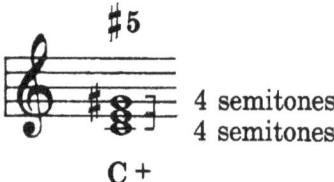

To learn to write and recognise these chord types, students are advised to complete pages 69 and 70 of *Contemporary Theory Workbook* – Book 1 (Brandman).

DOUBLE SHARP and DOUBLE FLAT SIGNS

When reading and writing Diminished and Augmented chords you will frequently encounter Double Sharp and Double Flat signs.

A Double Sharp sign is a small cross (𝄪) and a Double Flat sign is simply two flats next to each other (♭♭). They raise or lower the note by a Whole Tone.

To cancel either sign a single Natural sign is still used. However, if you want to bring them back to the single sharpened or flattened version of the note, in the same bar, both a **Natural Sign** and a **Single Sharp** or **Flat** must be used. Thus: ♮♯ or ♮♭.

THE COMPLETE MAJOR TABLE

The Table Of Chords. This can now be extended to include the triad built on the seventh degree of the scale which is the Diminished Triad. The Table for a Major Key should look like this:

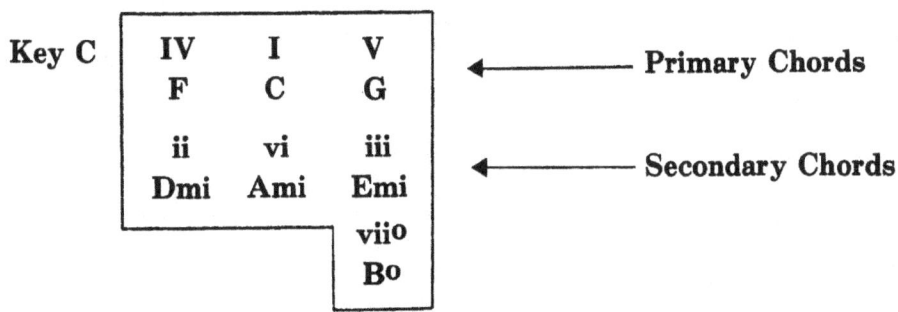

Music Speed-Reading
Interval Climbers - OCTAVES

Play in the same manner as the first three climbing exercises. Start on any note.

No. 4 OCTAVES

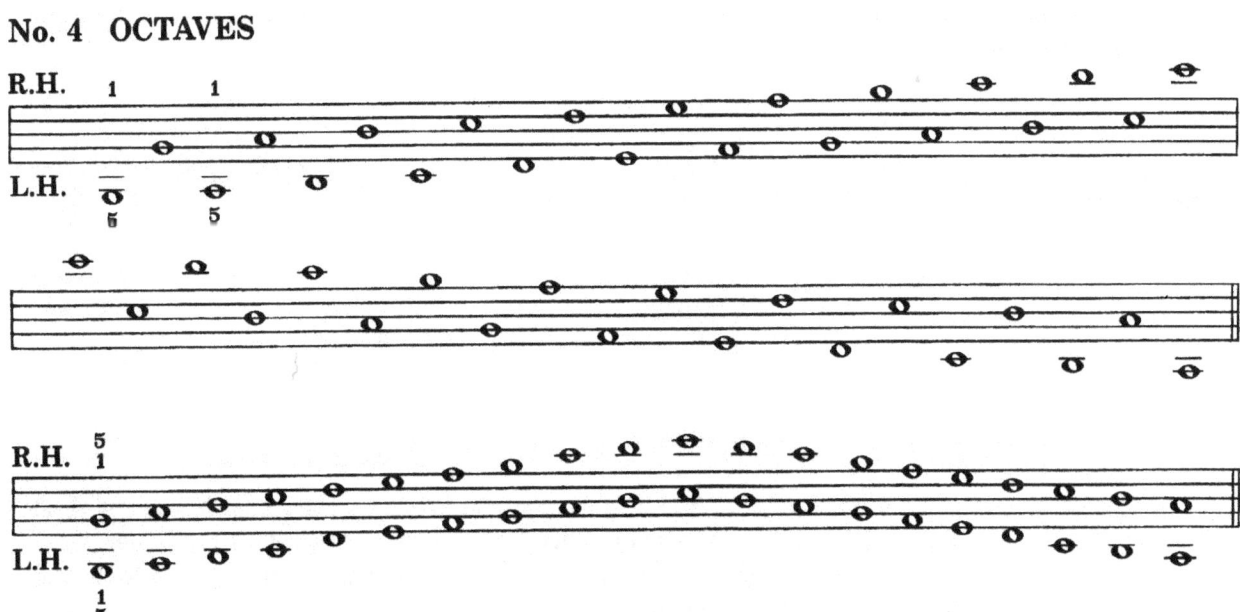

MINOR SCALES: Cm and Fm

C MINOR SCALE

C **Minor** is related to E flat Major and therefore has three flats: B, E, A. Play the Natural minor first and then raise the seventh note from B flat to B natural to convert the scale to the Harmonic Minor form.

F MINOR SCALE

F minor is related to A flat Major. It therefore has four flats: B, E, A, D. After playing the Natural minor, raise the seventh degree from E flat to E natural to play the Harmonic Form. The right hand fingering in this scale is the same as F Major that is: 1 2 3 4 1 2 3 4.

C AND F MINOR CHORDS

Form the minor triads of C and F minor by taking the first third and fifth degrees of the scales. C minor will be: C, E♭, G and F minor triad will be: F, A♭, C. Play these chords in the form given for the previous triads.

CONTRARY MOTION SCALES (B, D and G minor)

Add to the Contrary Minor scales of A and E the previously learnt Harmonic Minors of B, D and G. Again watch for the pattern of white against black and black against black that emerges as these scales are played in Contrary Motion. Remember to play the right hand up and back and then the left hand down and up before playing hands together.

TECHNIQUE TIP

In order to play thirds in which **one note** is repeated, in a legato manner, shorten the note that is to be repeated by approximately half its value, so that the repeated note can be struck cleanly. Take care to sustain the held note for its full value and connect it smoothly to the following notes.

THUS:

Written   Played

9. ROCKIN' THE BEAT ALONG

COMPLETE THE CHORD TABLE

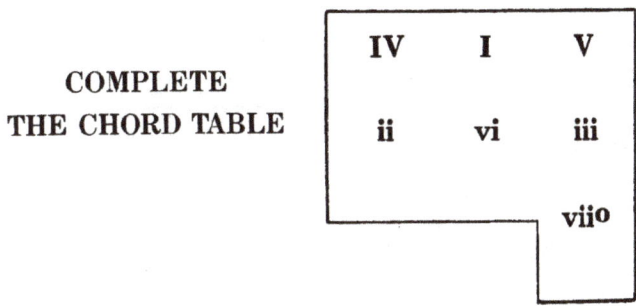

Write the Chord names above each bar.   Simile = continue in the same manner.

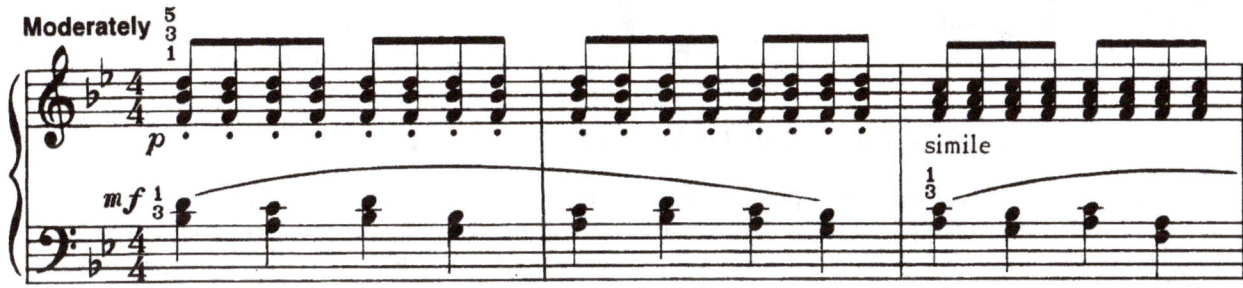

LEFT - HAND ACCOMPANIMENTS

If you refer to the section in Book 1 on this subject, you will recall that Style 2, used the Root and Fifth Notes as Bass notes on the first and third beats in 4/4 time, with the chords played in the middle register of the keyboard on beats two and four. A further development of the style is to use the **Third** degree also as a Bass Note. The Third degree is useful in extended sections on one chord (more than 2 bars), to provide variety, or when used as a leading note to the next Bass note of a different chord.

For Example:

Other variations that can be added to the basic style include using an ascending or descending scale run to link the Bass notes of two chords, instead of playing chords on beats 2 and 4.

For Example:

If an extra note is needed to make the connection, one of the notes can be repeated or a Chromatic passing note can be inserted.

For Example:

FURTHER DEVELOPMENTS FROM THIS STYLE

This style of accompaniment provides a good starting point for the development of other types of Left-Hand accompaniments. When divided into its components, the CHORDAL section, can be played on its own, with the Bass notes omitted altogether, and a more rhythmic treatment of the chords can be applied.

For Example:

The BASS part can be played on its own with the chords being omitted. This can be developed into a **Walking Bass Line** with the addition of more and more linking notes.

For Example:

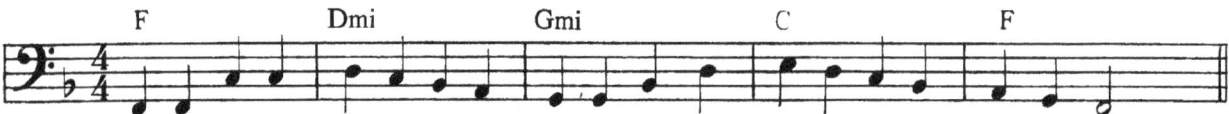

Alternatively, the Bass Part can be taken by the Left Hand while the Right Hand plays the Chords under the Right Hand melody line. If there is another instrument or voice available to take the melody line, the pianist plays the Bass Line in the Left Hand and the chords in the Right.

See examples on pages 88, 92, 99 and 151 — 152.

10. SONGBIRD

Add a left hand accompaniment to this piece, first in style one (close chords) and then in style two (stride bass)

COMPLETE THE CHORD TABLE

IV	I	V
ii	vi	iii
		vii°

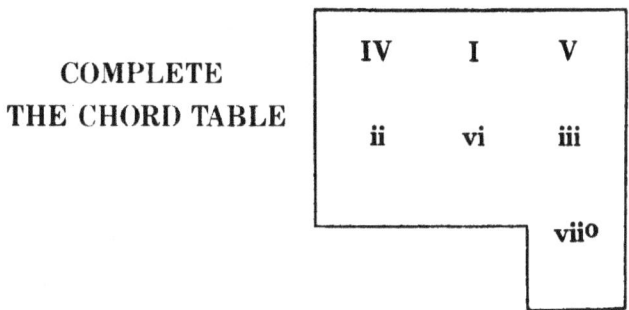

Moderato

Words and Music by Margaret Brandman

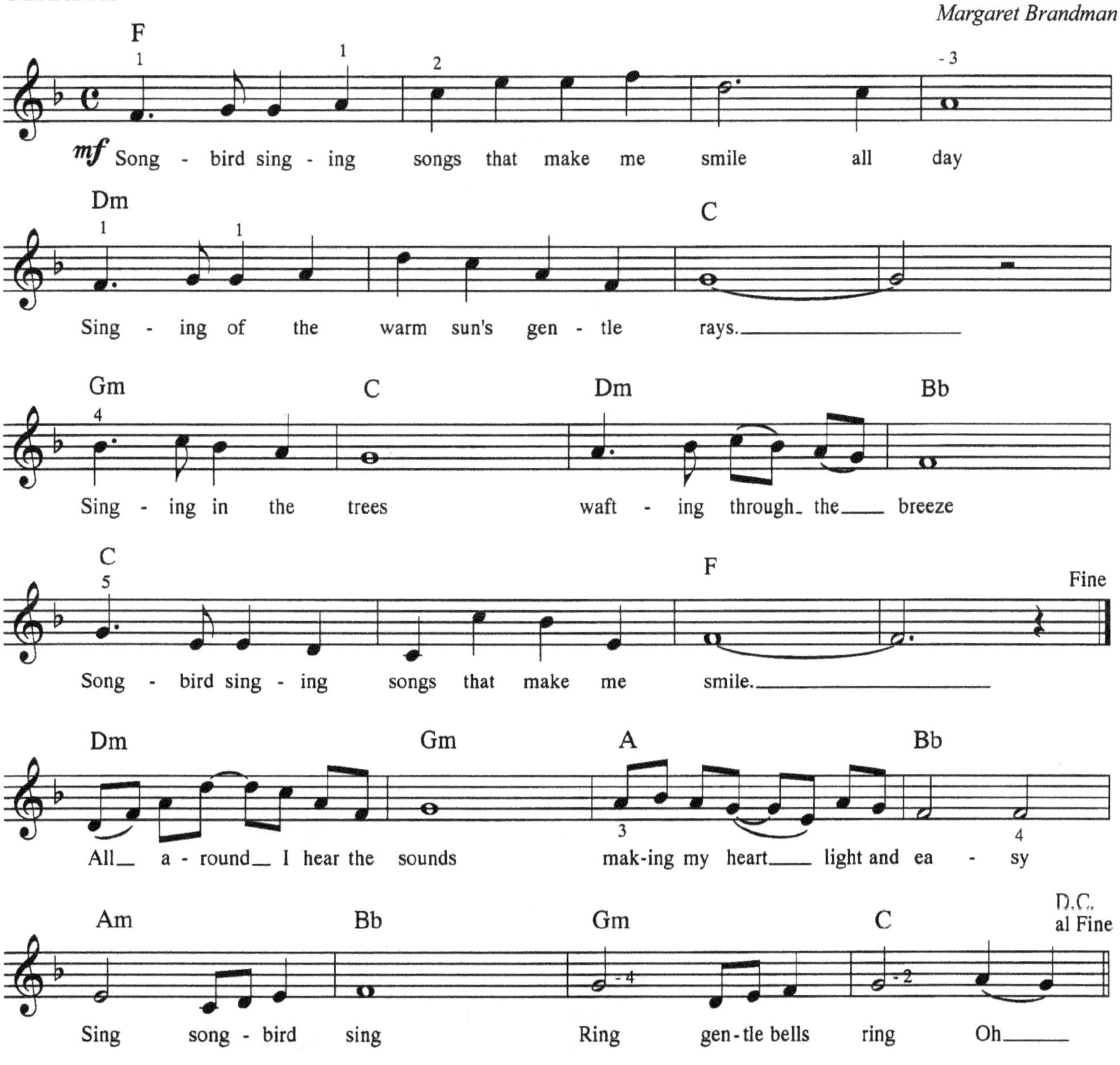

F
mf Song - bird sing - ing songs that make me smile all day
Dm
C
Sing - ing of the warm sun's gen - tle rays.
Gm
C
Dm
Bb
Sing - ing in the trees waft - ing through the breeze
C
F
Fine
Song - bird sing - ing songs that make me smile.
Dm
Gm
A
Bb
All a - round I hear the sounds mak-ing my heart light and ea - sy
Am
Bb
Gm
C
D.C. al Fine
Sing song - bird sing Ring gen-tle bells ring Oh

Refer to *'Its Easy to Improvise'* (Brandman) to expand your skills. This book contains more suggestions for Left Hand accompaniments, ideas for right hand embellishment and improvisation and songs in to which to apply them.

THE MINOR KEY, CHORD TABLE

To construct a **table** for a **Minor Key**, the triads on both the Harmonic and Melodic Minor scales must be worked out. See example 1 for the triads on A Minor Scale (both forms).

Example 1.

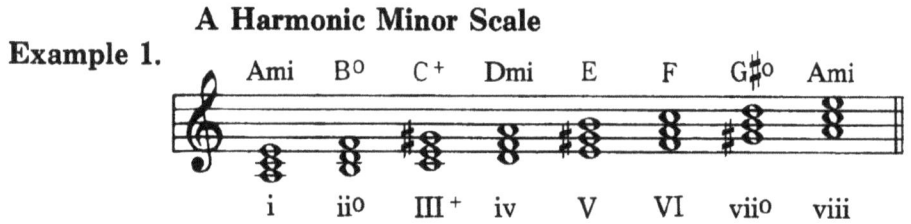

A Harmonic Minor Scale

(Small numerals — minor or diminished
Large numerals — Major or Augmented)

A Melodic Minor Scale

The **table is a composite** of the most commonly used Triads in an actual piece of music in a Minor key. The Minor Table looks like this:

KEY: C Minor

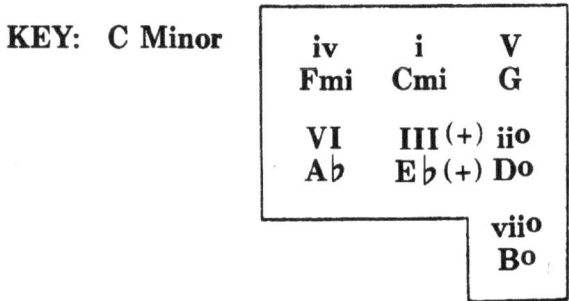

Note that the Dominant Chord is Major in both Major and Minor Keys. In the Minor Key this is due to the **raised seventh** in the Harmonic Form.

As explained on page 24, the chords must be written above and below one another so it can be clearly seen that one chord may substitute for the other.

Remember, to find the Key of a piece, first look at the Key Signature and then check to see what the lowest note in the Bass and what the final chord in the piece is. The final chord and in particular the Bass note of that chord will give you the Tonic of the piece and tell you whether it is a Major or Minor Key. If you think the piece is in a Minor Key, double check by looking for accidentals in the body of the piece indicating a raised seventh. Then write the Table accordingly.

The fingers will only be able to find the right notes if the mind knows the construction of the piece and is aware of what to expect.

11. NIGHT FLYING

COLOUR AND CLAP

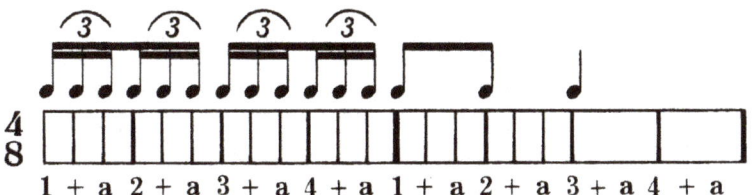

TRIPLET — Count: 1+a 2+a 3+a 4+a

COMPLETE THE CHORD TABLE

KEY: A Minor

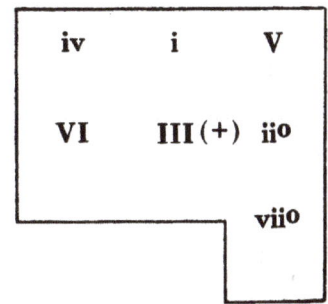

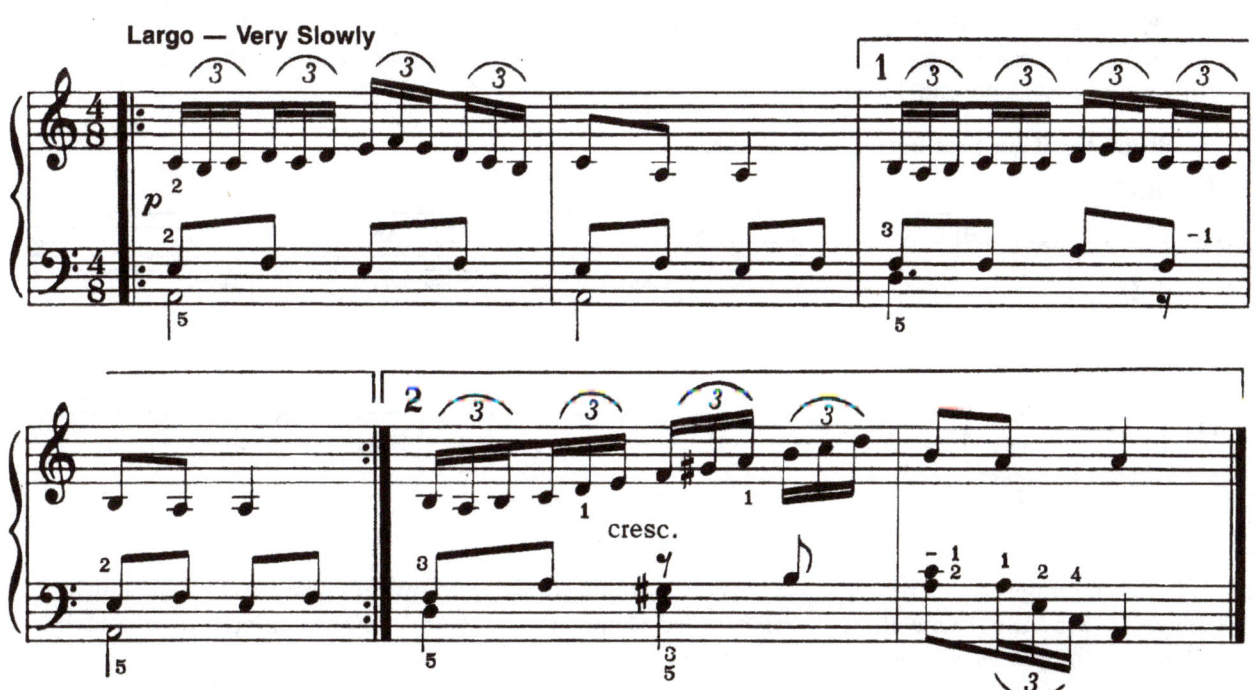

Music Speed-Reading
Root position tetrad shapes and octave spans

These exercises require the hand to be set over the Octave span. As a result several of the intervals have to be handled by finger extensions.

In the first two lines (1a and 1b) the distance of a 4th (skip-plus-one) can be judged in the usual fashion but the 5th (jump) requires a stretch. This should be easy to do if you have your hand spanning the Octave and you take your bearings from that position.

⌐¬ — extension (stretch fingers)

Exercises 2a and 2b require the 5th to be judged by extending the 2nd finger (previously used for the distance of a 4th).

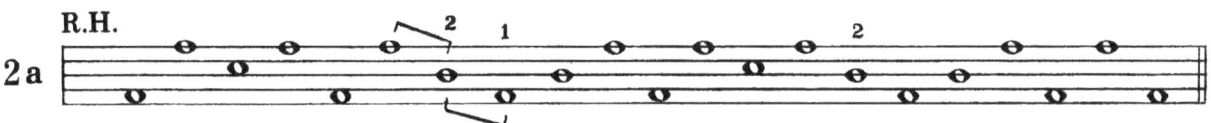

Exercises 3a and 3b use the 4-note chord shape in Root Position. The Right Hand uses extensions between each finger and the Left Hand uses extensions between the 5th and 4th fingers and the 2nd and 1st fingers.

Root Position four-note chord shape.

When applying this procedure to pieces, read ahead and sum up the music to see how much is playable with the 4-note Root Position chord shape. You will find many instances of this chord shape in the pieces you play particularly in the music of J. S. Bach.

Practise these shapes on all Major and Minor chords, even those that start on Black Keys. The fingering is the same for all keys except for the Left Hand in the Keys of D, A, E, B and F sharp Majors. In those keys use the 3rd finger instead of the 4th.

READING INTERVALS ACROSS THE GREAT STAFF

The Leger Line on which Middle "C" is written, is an Eleventh line between the two sets of 5 lines used for the Bass and Treble Clefs.

Taking this into consideration, thirds, fifths and sevenths are still written from line to line or from space to space, and seconds, fourths, sixths and octaves are still written from line to space or vice-versa, even though the visual distance is greater owing to the separation of the Treble and Bass Staves.

See the Example Below.

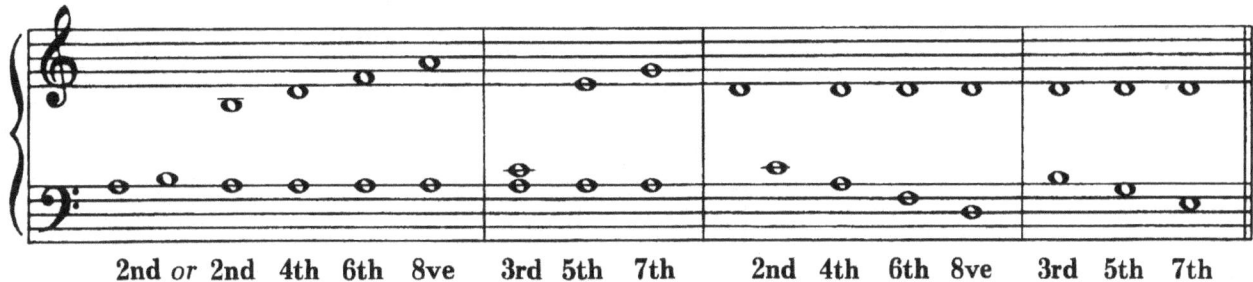

M.M. This is an abbreviation for Maelzel's Metronome and will be followed by ♩ = 120 etc. This indicates the number of pulses per minute. For instance ♩ = 60 means one beat per second.

Metronomes are currently available in both Pendulum and Electronic models. A Metronome is a very useful study aid and should be part of any musician's equipment.

THE ARPEGGIANDO SIGN

An Arpeggio is a chord played over one or more octaves in the form of separate notes following each other. Therefore, the ARPEGGIANDO sign means play each note separately from the lowest note upwards holding each one down for its full length once depressed. The sound is similar to that of a Harp or Guitar.

If the direction of the Arpeggiando is to be reversed, a small arrow indicating the direction is added to the sign. Thus:

12. WALKIN' EASY

COLOUR AND CLAP

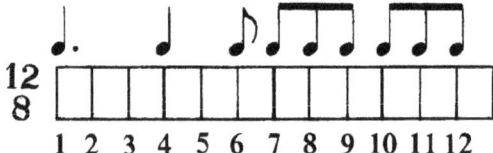

COMPLETE THE CHORD TABLE

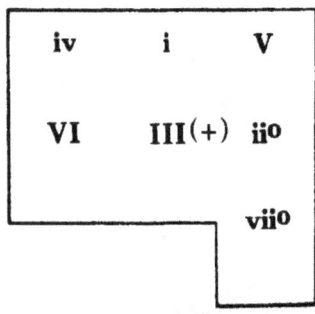

WALKIN' EASY

13. HAVA NAGILA

This is a popular Hebrew folk-tune, the melody of which is taken from the Harmonic Minor Scale. Complete the Chord Table and write the chords above each bar before playing this tune.

CHORD TABLE

Arranged by M. S. Brandman

51

DOMINANT SEVENTH CHORDS

This type of seventh chord is the most frequently used so it is wise to learn all of them as soon as possible.

You will have already seen that a triad can be built on each note of the scale. These can be extended to sevenths by combining the 1st, 3rd, 5th and 7th notes from any starting note. You should also know the degree names of the notes of the scale, (see page 32, Book 1). Thus if a seventh is built on the first note of the scale it is a Tonic Seventh; on the second note — a Supertonic Seventh and so on. As the Fifth Degree of the scale is known as the "dominant" the seventh built on that note must be the Dominant Seventh Chord.

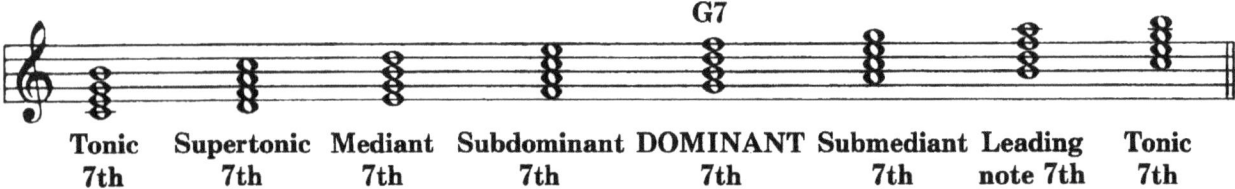

The function of this chord is to lead back to the Tonic Chord. Play the G seventh chord and follow it with the closest C Major triad you can find. Listen to the strong pull from the first chord (7th) to the next (tonic). The G seventh will also have the same effect in C minor. (Owing to the Raised Seventh in the Harmonic Minor scale the Dominant Seventh chord is the same in both Major and Minor keys).

When you look for a Dominant Seventh in a piece, the most common place to find it is as the second last chord in the piece.

The example below shows five Dominant Sevenths in the keys they belong to. Note that in Modern Music we refer to the Dominant Seventh by its note name and the player is expected to know to which key it belongs.

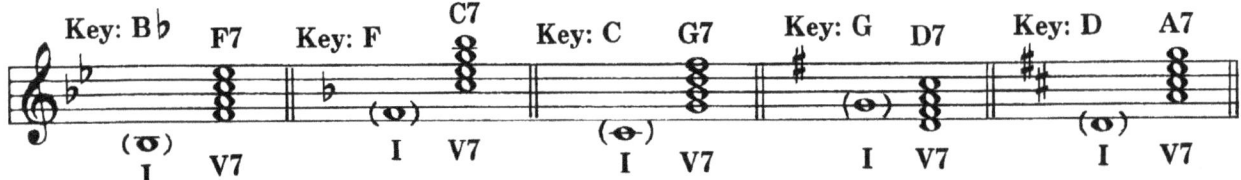

Practical Exercise

Resolve each of these Dominant 7th chords to the nearest inversion of the Tonic Major or Tonic Minor chord. Refer to page 40 of *Pictorial Patterns for Keyboard Scales and Chords* for further suggestions on chord progression incorporating this type of seventh chord.

Anyone with classical training will have to differentiate between this and the way Classical Theorists refer to the chord being the Dominant Seventh of a certain key. The next example shows G seventh chord with its inversions which should be practised in block and broken form. The basic fingering for sevenths is with 1 and 5 on the outer two notes and the comfortable fingerings in between ... either 2 and 3 or 2 and 4. Practise all five Dominant sevenths in this manner.

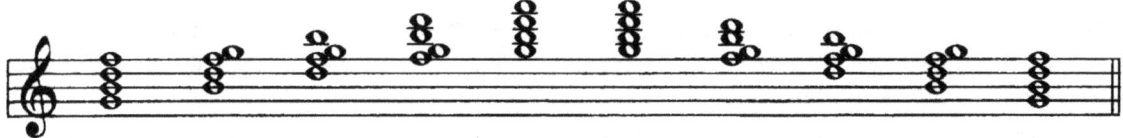

USING THE DOMINANT SEVENTH CHORD IN THE TABLE

The Table. It would be useful at this stage to refer to V in the table as a **Dominant seventh** as the seventh is used in the majority of cases. Write the table out with a small 7 next to the 5th degree thus: IV, I, V7.

In Modern Sheet music and Jazz Notation the "7" on its own is always taken to mean Dominant Seventh because of the fact that this form of seventh is the most common. (The Tonic Seventh, and Supertonic sevenths are different again as you will see in the following pages).

When you are learning these seventh chords there are two other ways to remember them. **Firstly,** learn the distances between the degrees: from 1 to 3 is four semitones, from 3 to 5 is three semitones, and from 5 to 7 is three semitones. **Secondly,** you can build a Dominant seventh from any note by playing a Major chord and adding a Minor Seventh interval to it.

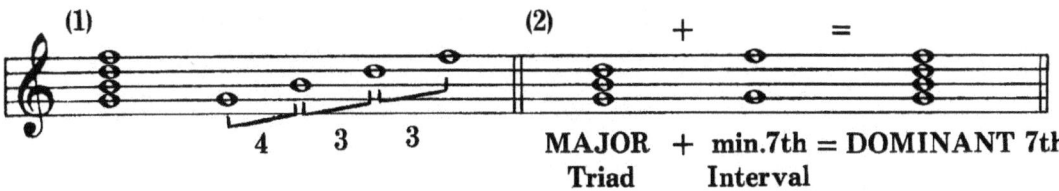

To learn to write and recognise the Dominant Seventh chords students are advised to complete pages 35 and 38 of *Contemporary Theory Workbook – Book 2* (Brandman) and pages 33 -37 of *Contemporary Chord Workbook – Book 1* (Brandman).

ORNAMENTS

The ornaments described on the following pages are a representative selection of the most commonly used ornamental figures found up to the present day. Many variations in the interpretation of these signs occur and the execution of the sign depends on the performer's knowledge of the composer's intention, or failing that, the editorial footnotes on the printed music.

So as to simplify this subject, I have chosen the generally accepted interpretation of the sign and provided an example of how it can be played. Where the section is marked with an asterisk, other variations can be found.

If the student wishes to study the subject in depth, there is a wealth of material available on the subject and new 'Theses' on the subject can be found in most major music dictionaries.

Acciaccatura
The small note with the line through its stem. Also known as a GRACE note or CRUSHED note. Played with the smaller note "crushed" onto the following note.

14. GRASSHOPPER HOP

THE EXTENDED MINOR KEY CHORD TABLE

The brackets show alternative chord choices for each degree.
Keep these chord choices in mind when analysing this piece.

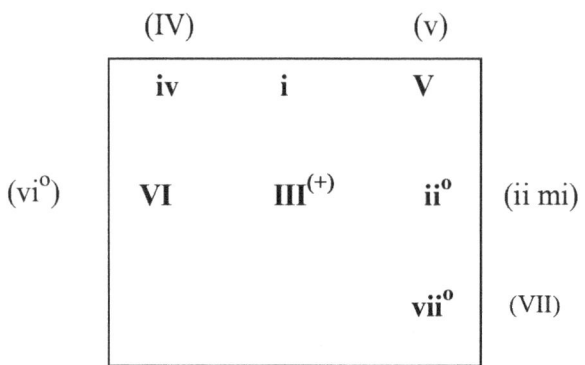

GRASSHOPPER HOP

Clap the timing of each separate stave before playing this piece.

PEDALLING

The most effective and commonly used style of pedalling is SYNCOPATED PEDALLING. Syncopation when applied to timing means the deliberate upsetting of the natural beat. When it is applied to pedalling it means a similar thing, in that the pedal is depressed AFTER the note (beat), **not** at the same time.

The Pedal I am referring to at this stage is the Right Hand pedal — The Sustain Pedal. The effect of this pedal is to hold on to the note, even when the hand is lifted off the keyboard, while at the same time making the note sound fuller. Do **not** make the mistake of thinking that the note is therefore louder as well. (Some people erroneously call this pedal the Loud Pedal).

The Left Pedal is the Soft or Dampening Pedal, see page 119 and if there is a third pedal in the centre, it can function in one of two ways; it can either be a "Practice Pedal" which dampens the sound even more than the Soft Pedal and usually "locks in" on a ledge so that it can stay down all the time and your neighbours will be left in peace. This pedal is usually found on upright models only. **OR,** this centre pedal when found on a Grand Piano or a more expensive Upright Model, functions as a "Sustain Pedal" for the lower half of the piano only, so that one can sustain a Bass Note and have several changes of harmony over it, pedalled normally with the Right Pedal.

Returning now to the Right Hand (foot) Sustain Pedal: when playing this pedal it is advisable to keep one's heel on the floor and shoes with a small amount of heel make this easier than playing with scuffs, etc. As mentioned before the Pedal should go down **after** the note. Look inside the piano for the reason. When this pedal is depressed, all the dampers lift up and therefore all the strings are able to vibrate. If you have the pedal down at the same time as the hammer hits the strings, all other strings with sympathetic vibrations will be set into motion and the result will be a very jumbled sound. However, if you strike the note you want first and then depress the pedal, only the strings of that particular note will continue to vibrate and you will get a cleaner sound.

See page 57 for the Four Steps to successful pedalling.

Special Note on the Centre Pedal

The Sustain Pedal for the lower half of the piano is found on North American pianos. The 'Sostenuto' Pedal, which sustains any note, or group of notes throughout the range of the piano, while allowing other notes to be played without sustain, is found mainly on European pianos, and in particular in Grand pianos.

Step 1. Depress the pedal to start, for the purpose of this exercise. Next, play the exercise very slowly, in strict time. Play the note on beat one and hold it throughout the bar. Meanwhile, lift the pedal on beat two (this clears the previous sound) and replace the pedal on beat three (this catches the new note). Repeat this process until it becomes comfortable and natural on the notes in the five finger position given. As you go, say: Note — Up — Down, Note — Up — Down, etc.

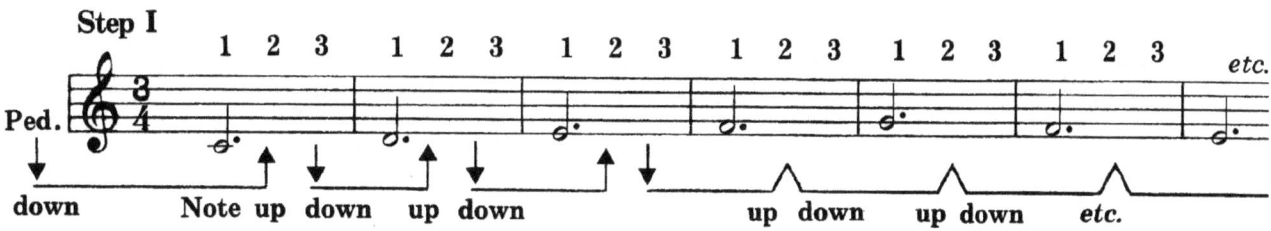

Step 2. This exercise brings the pedalling process established in Step 1 a little closer together. After each note lift and then depress the pedal before moving on to the next note. (Remember to start this exercise with the pedal down first also).

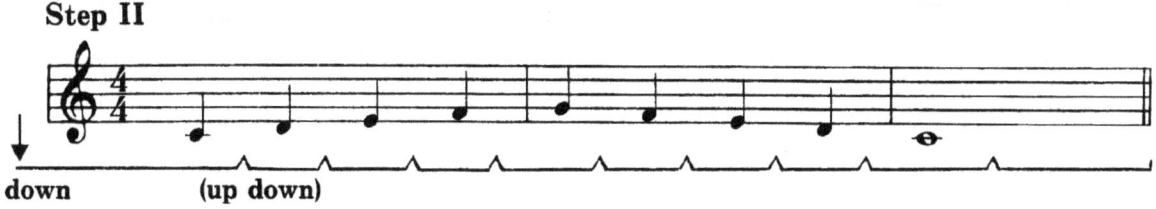

Step 3. When applying this technique in normal playing situations, the pedal is usually applied after the first note has been struck, and from there on the pedalling is the same as the previous exercise.

Step 4. You will find pedalling usually is used in order to bind together notes of the same chord. It is usually cleared therefore, after the first note of each new chord. This is another field in which your knowledge of chords is essential for good pedalling when there is none marked.

CHORD AND PEDAL STUDY IN D MAJOR

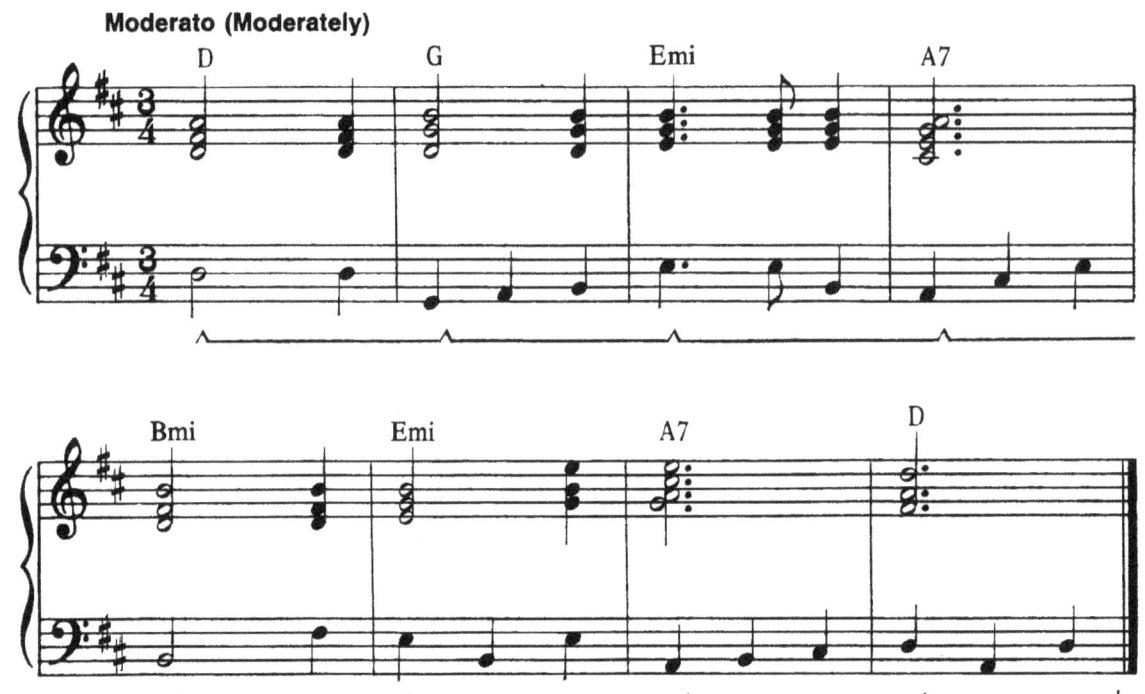

* **Appoggiatura**

The small note takes half the value of the following note.
(**Note:** NO line through the stem of the small note).

Technique Tip: When playing the above, place a little more weight on the first note (the appoggiatura) and lessen the weight on the second note. Connect the two notes smoothly.

The "TIMES SIGN":

In music the mathematical sign for multiplication, the "X", is used as a short hand way to say "TIME" in the context of "First Time", "Second Time", etc. For instance, "Play First Time only" can be written "Play 1st X Only".

15. FALLING LEAVES

COMPLETE THE CHORD TABLE

iv	i	V7
VI	III (+)	ii°
		vii°

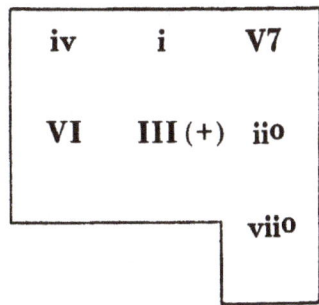

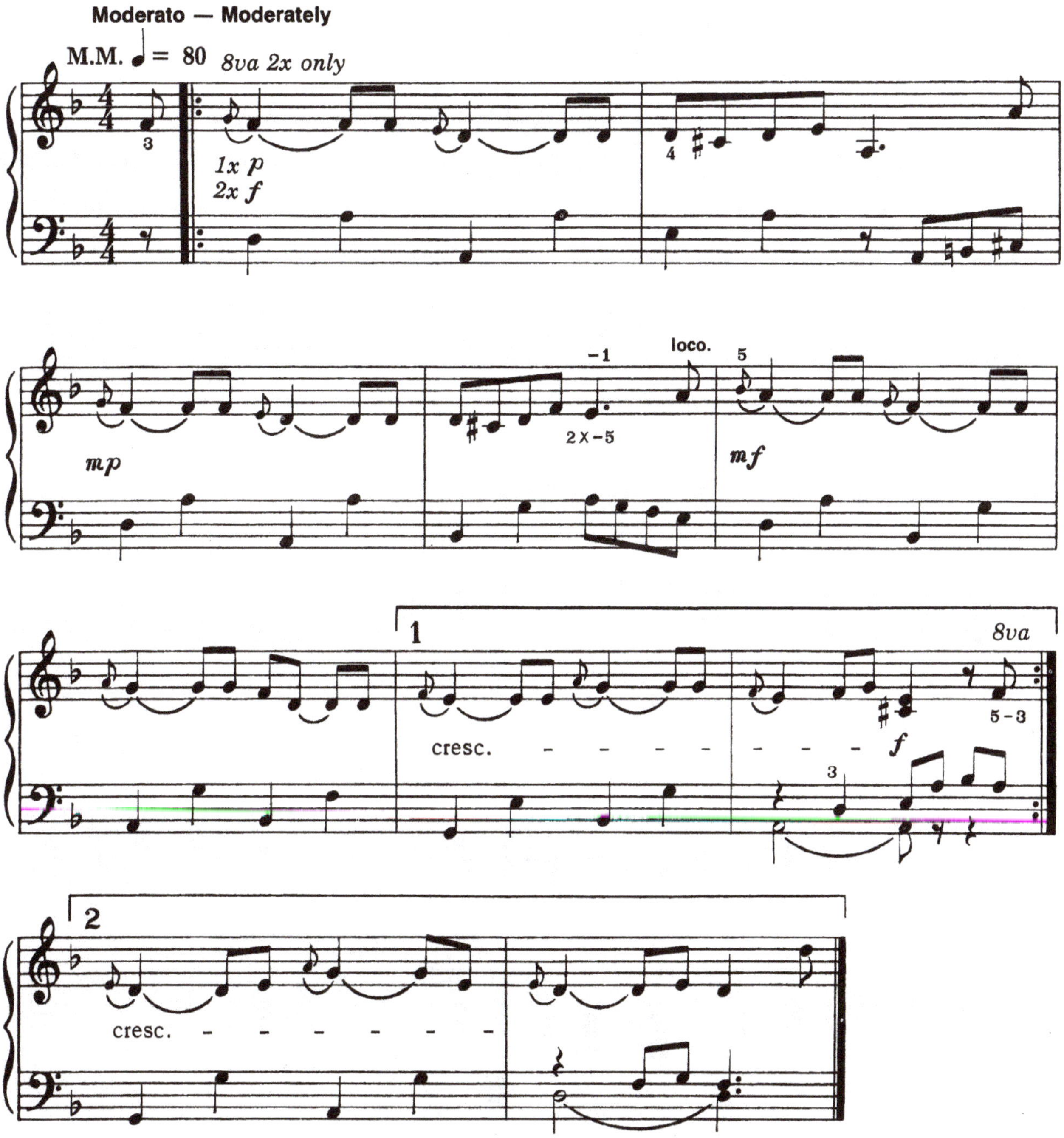

Music Speed-Reading
New position changing methods - 2
Chord Climbing using Root Position triads

As in the interval climbing exercises given earlier in this book, these chord climbing exercises require a shift of hand-position. Place the correct finger on the marked position (where a "1" or "5" is indicated) and adjust the chord position in relation to this finger.

Play these Chord Climbing exercises on:
1. any white note as starting note;
2. on all the Major triads starting on white notes, adding the correct sharps for each chord; and
3. on all Minor triads starting on white notes, with the correct sharps or flats for each chord.
4. Transposed into the Major and Minor keys that you are familiar with, using the sharps or flats of the particular key you have chosen.

BROKEN CHORD STYLE

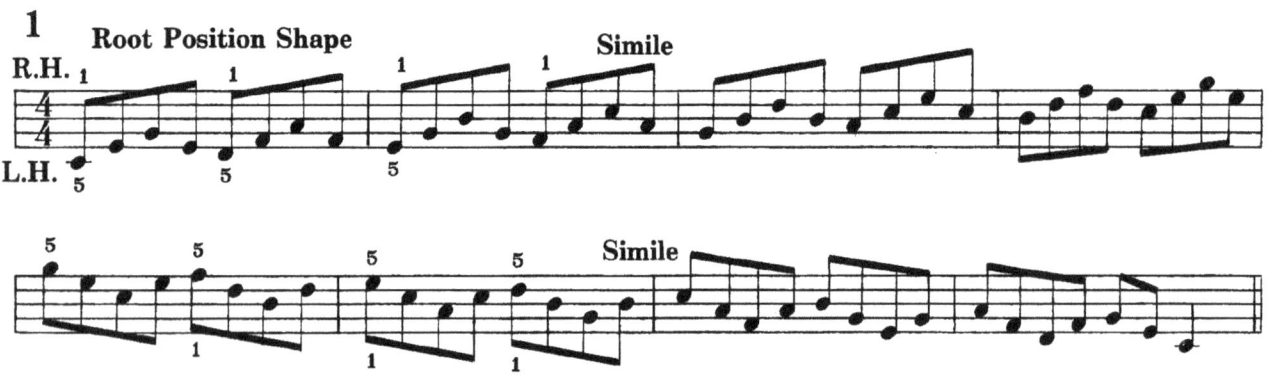

BLOCK CHORD STYLE

16. OLD DANCE TUNE

CHORD TABLE

HENRY PURCELL, 1659–1695
English
Early Baroque Style

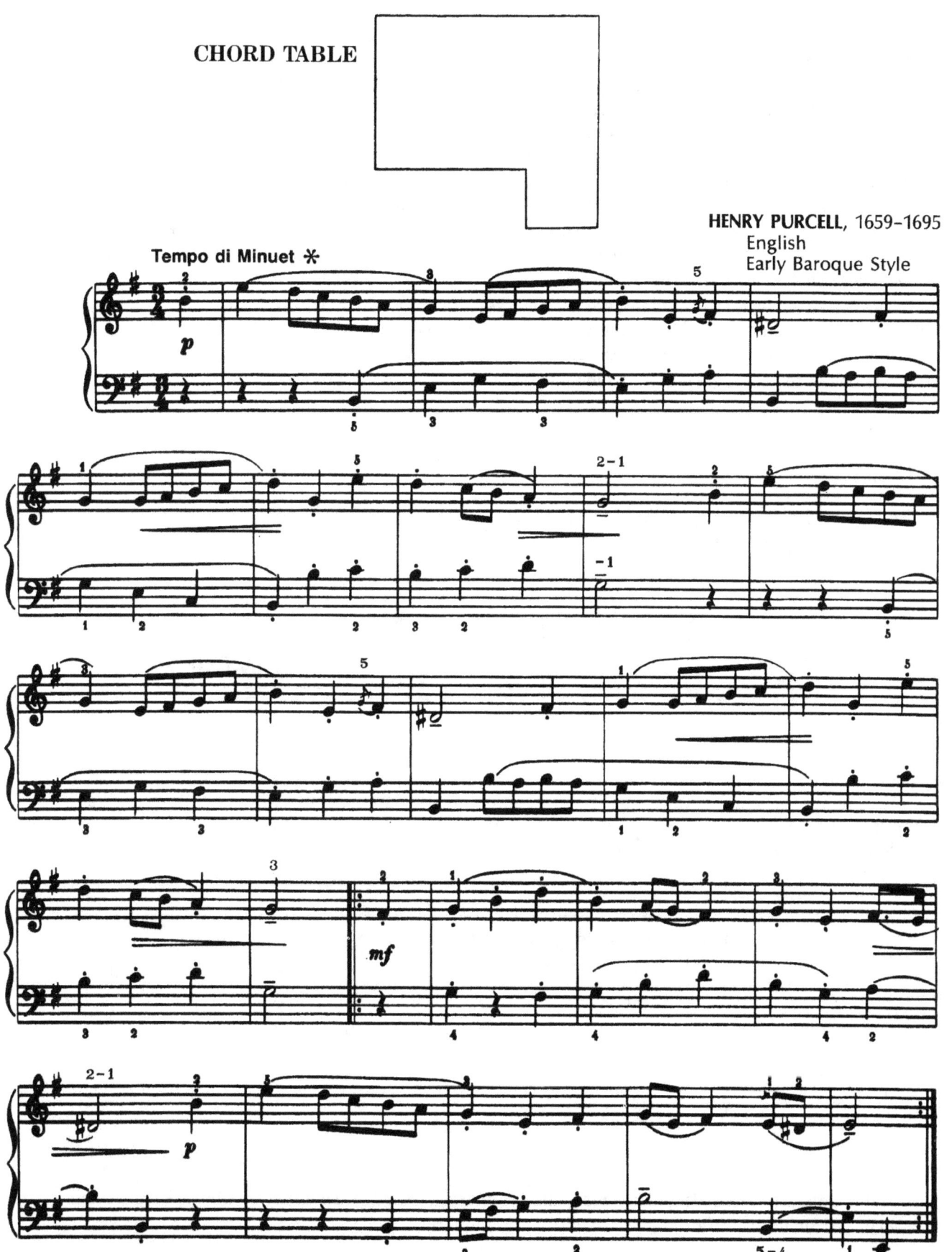

*A Minuet is a graceful French dance which was popular in England and Europe in the 17th and 18th Centuries. The name comes from the French word "menu" meaning small and refers to the small steps taken by the dancers. The music is played at a moderate pace.

CHORD NAMING SYSTEMS

There are **two** ways of indicating a chord and its inversions.

1. The first method is by **"Figuring"** the chord. This means identifying the chord by its degree number in the scale and identifying the inversion by the intervals between the notes. This system, often known as the **"Figured Bass"** system, was widely used by composers of the 17th and 18th centuries. Only the bass part was written for the keyboard player (the keyboard was either a Harpsichord or a Clavichord, the piano had not yet been invented). The bass part was the same as the line played by the 'cello player. The keyboard player was required to supply the chords indicated, above the bass part. This process was called "Realising" the figured bass.

These days the system provides musicians with a handy way of indicating the inversions of a triad or 7th chord. For instance, a First Inversion chord is marked $\frac{6}{3}$ because of the fact that the intervals from the bass note are a 6th and a 3rd.

The type of chord, major, minor, etc, was worked out from which degree of the scale the chord was built on. For instance, if the chord was built on the second degree of the Major Scale, it would then be a minor chord. (See the Chord Table for a Major Key).

See below for the figuring for triads and 7ths.

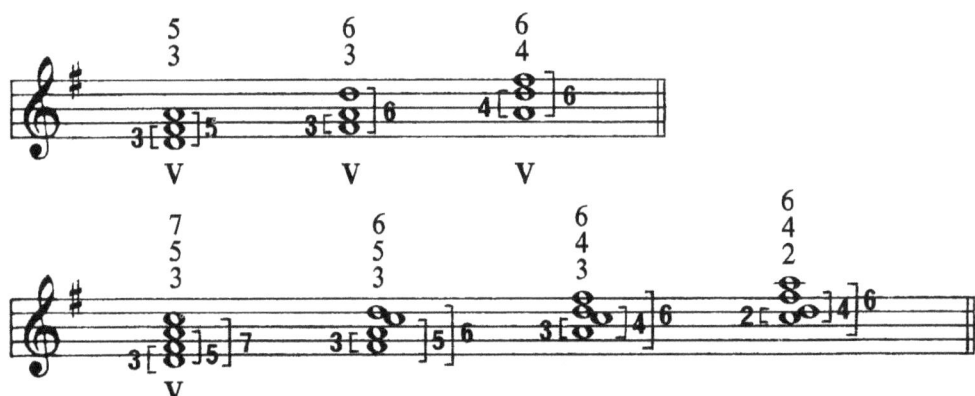

These numbers are further simplified by taking all the numbers of the Root Position triad as being understood. As well, several other numbers for the other inversions are also taken to be understood. These numbers are marked with brackets.

TRIADS	Root	1st Inv.	2nd Inv.	SEVENTHS	Root	1st Inv.	2nd Inv.	3rd Inv.
	(5)	6	6		7	6	(6)	(6)
	(3)	(3)	4		(5)	5	4	4
					(3)	(3)	3	2
Thus the standard system is:	—	6	6 4		7	6 5	4 3	4 2

If a note has to be altered to create an Augmented chord or Diminished Chord, etc, a small sharp, flat or natural sign is placed next to the numeral.

For Example: $I\,\substack{\sharp 5 \\ 3}$ or $I\,\substack{6 \\ \sharp 3}$.

MODERN CHORD SYMBOLS

2. The second way of indicating a chord and its inversion is the **Modern Chord naming system,** which has been the system used in this book up to this point. The name of the chord is supplied with the appropriate additions for the minor, diminished and augmented triads.

Thus far, we have seen the Major Triad indicated by its letter name only (e.g. F); the minor triad indicated by its letter name followed by a small "mi" (e.g. Fmi); the diminished triad indicated by a small circle after the letter name (e.g. F°); and the augmented triad indicated by a small plus-sign after the letter name, (e.g. F+).

As seen on the previous pages the Dominant 7th chord is indicated by the number 7 only. As you move through this book the other types of 7ths and the ways to indicate them will be discussed.

To indicate which inversion is to be played, which also generally means which note has to be played in the Bass Part, the name of the bass note is written under the chord name. Thus, C major triad in first inversion would be indicated; C/E.

If the composer wishes to indicate the specific Right Hand chord shape only, the figuring system is once again used.

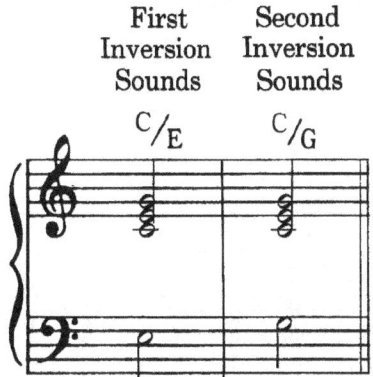

Music Speed-Reading
Chord Climbing using First Inversion triads

1. Play the following Chord Climbing Exercises using any white note as a starting position.
2. If you have practised the Major and Minor triads on the keys of F, C, G, D, A, E and B try these exercises, playing each chord position as 1. a Major triad; and 2. a Minor triad in the appropriate inversion.
3. Transposed into the Major and Minor keys that you are familiar with, using the sharps or flats of the particular key you have chosen.

Arranging
The two tunes on the following page are in minor keys and make use of both minor chords and Dominant 7th chords. Add a left hand accompaniment in Style One (see CPM Book 1A) keeping the chords in close position, using nearby inversions of the following chords.

ARRANGING SONGS WITH MINOR CHORDS AND DOMINANT SEVENTH CHORDS

The Wraggle Taggle Gypsies, O!

This song is in the Aeolian Mode on D, also known as D Natural Minor.

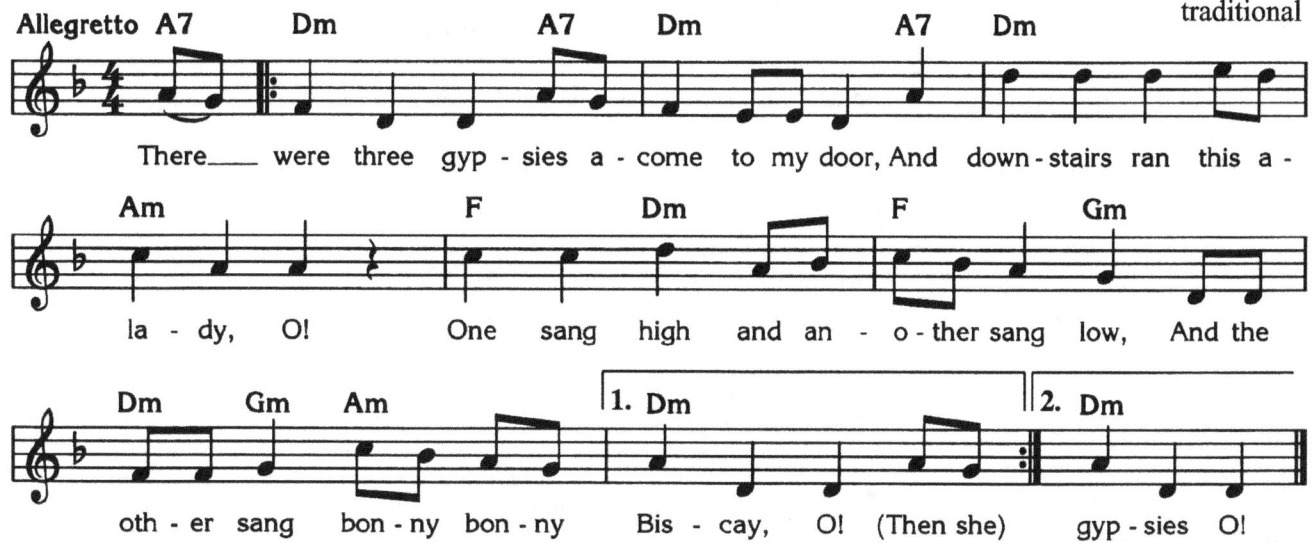

When Johnny Comes Marching Home

Sound the chords in the same rhythm as the melody in bar two.

THE SOUND OF INTERVALS

This lesson is concerned with differentiating between intervals by their sound.

PERFECT INTERVALS

If you refer to page 34 where the naming of intervals was discussed, you will see that *four* intervals come under the heading of "Perfect Intervals". These are the: Perfect Unison, Perfect 4th, Perfect 5th and Perfect 8th (Octave). Play each of these and note that the sound is rather "open" and "clear". (Fourths have an eastern sound rather like the sounds in Chinese and Japanese music, and Fifths have the type of sound that you hear in the Red Indian chants; refer to your favourite Western movie).

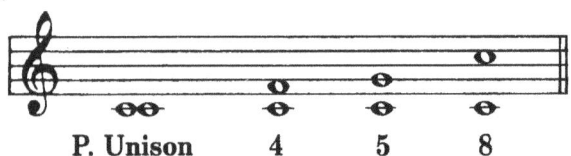

CONSONANT INTERVALS

Next you will notice that 3rds and 6ths (both major and minor) sound quite smooth and sweet. These are known as "Consonant" intervals. Consonant means sounding together, from "con" meaning "with" and "son" meaning sound.

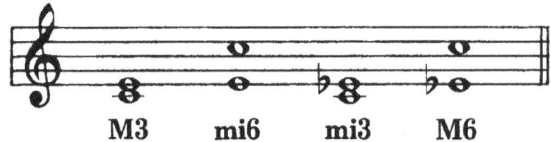

DISSONANT INTERVALS

The third group are the "Dissonant" intervals, 2nds and 7ths (major and minor). These are the opposite in sound to Consonant intervals. Dissonant means "sounding against". "Dis"=against and "son"=sound. Listen to them and you will hear the harsh, clashy quality that they have.

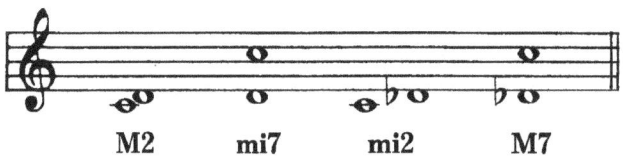

THE TRITONE

Lastly, there is one other interval which is also dissonant in sound but has a quality of its own. This is the Augmented 4th or Diminished 5th (same sounds) interval. It is also known as a "Tritone" as the distance is three tones. In Medieval Music it was known as the "devil in music", (Diabolus in Musica) and was avoided as much as possible.

It has, however, a very strong pull and is the key component of the Dominant 7th and Diminished 7th (and triad) chords.

Try to be aware of these sounds as you are playing and let your ear tell you if you are playing a wrong interval rather than looking at the keyboard to find out. This leaves your eyes free to continue checking out the next notes to be played.

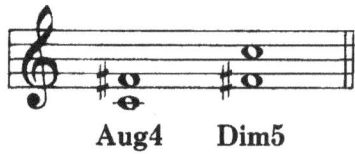

Music Speed-Reading

Chord Climbing using Second Inversion triads

Play the following Chord Climbing Exercises using any white note as a starting position. As suggested on page 60, try them as Major and Minor triads as well, and transposed into various keys.

SUSPENDED 4th CHORDS

A common chord found in much popular music is the Suspended 4th triad. This is a simple major triad with its 3rd degree being replaced by the 4th degree of the scale. When played it sounds as if the 4th is suspended in mid air. There is a strong downward pull which usually is resolved in the following chord. (The 4th moves down to the 3rd). The sound is often used in church music. See example a.

This example is arranged in Vocal Style. See note on page 95.

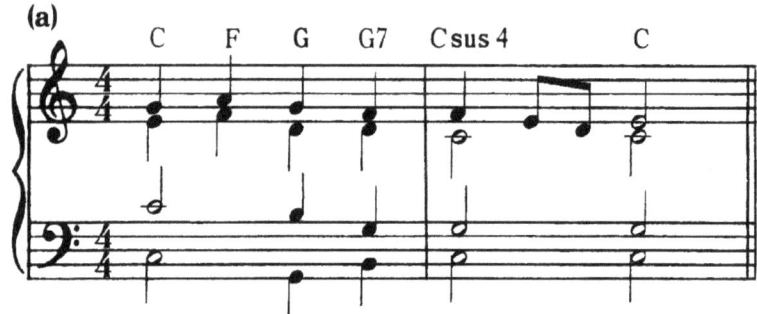

These days it is also a common sound in Disco and Funk music. See example b. As often as not, the chord is extended to a four-note chord using the flattened seventh degree as well. As such, it briefly replaces the Dominant 7th chord and usually resolves onto the complete Dominant 7th chord shortly after. This chord is usually written C7sus4 or just C7sus, the 4 being understood. See example c.

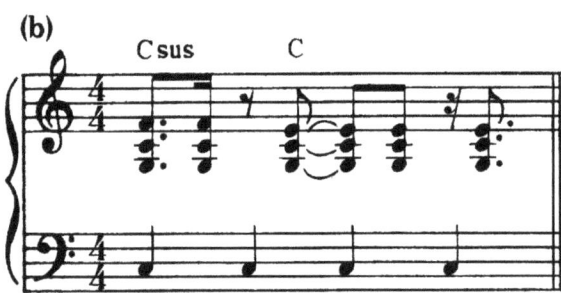

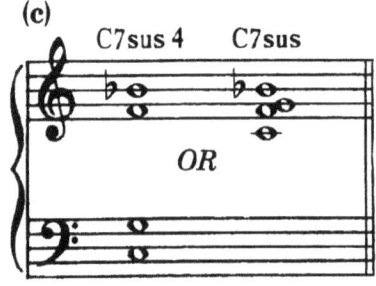

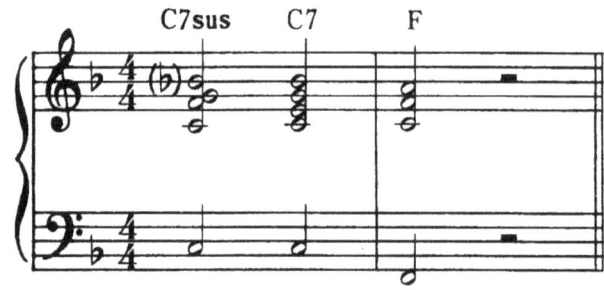

OSTINATO BASS

The word Ostinato is the Italian word for "obstinate" or "persistent". When applied to music it signifies a musical figure which is repeated unchanged throughout a section of a piece or sometimes for the whole tune.

Most often this figure is in the Bass part, hence the term "Ostinato Bass", but sometimes the Ostinato is found in the Treble or middle parts.

The English composer Henry Purcell (1658-1695) frequently used the device of the Ostinato Bass. One of the best known examples is the song "When I am laid in Earth" from the opera "Dido and Aeneas". See example 1.

EXAMPLE 1

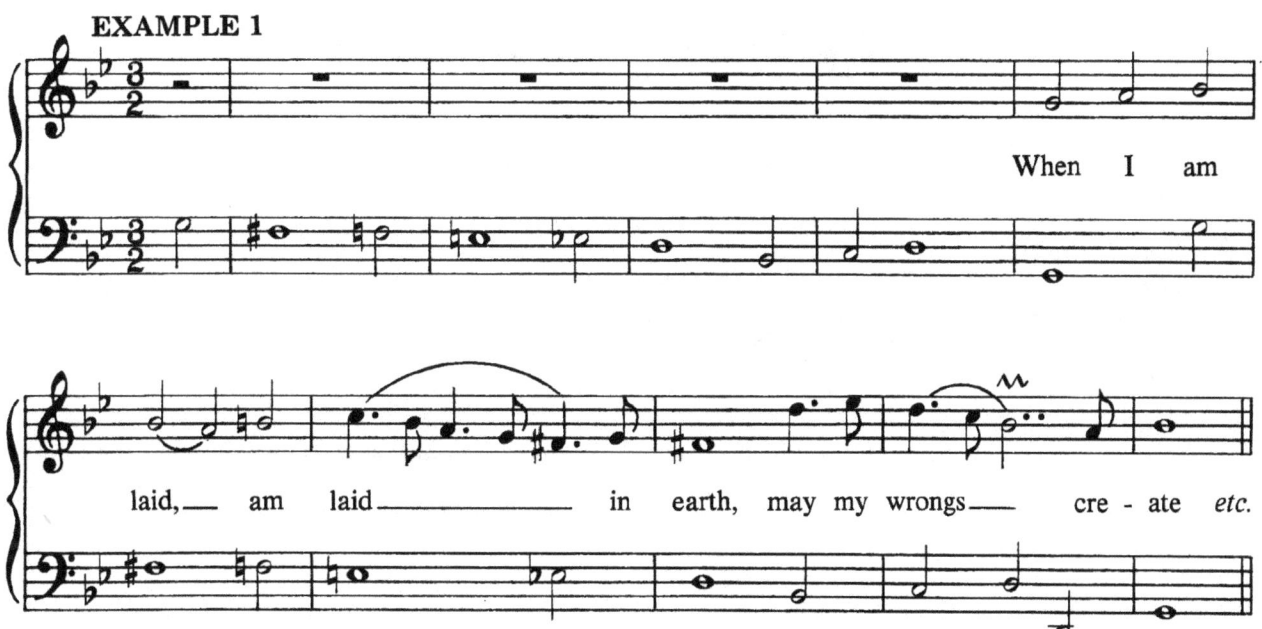

This type of Ostinato figure is also known as a "Ground Bass".

Listen also to the hypnotic effect of Maurice Ravel's Bolero, written in 1927, which sets up an Ostinato figure in the Bolero rhythm. See example 2.

EXAMPLE 2

In relation to popular music, the idea of the Ostinato Bass figure as a repeated Left Hand figure, is found in many Boogie-Woogie and Rock Tunes. The figures used are not strict "Ostinato" figures as they generally do not remain in one position throughout, being transposed onto the 4th and 5th degrees to suit the Chord Changes in the 12-Bar Blues, yet they have the same strength and set up the same pulsating foundation for the tunes. Below are the Ostinato figures for "Tell me What'd I Say", by Ray Charles and "Lucille" by Little Richard. In both these tunes the Bass figure is such an important ingredient that the songs would not be recognisable without the figures. See examples 3a and 3b.

Another perfect example of a tune written throughout on an Ostinato figure is Henry Mancini's "Peter Gunn". See example 4.

EXAMPLE 4

TRILL (Tr.)

Play the written note alternating with the one above, several times quickly. Take both notes from the scale of the piece, unless otherwise indicated.

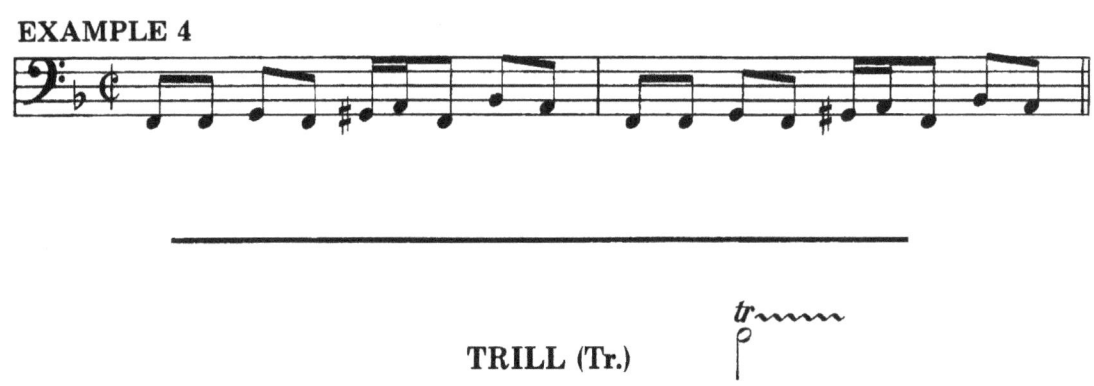

OR — beginning with an Acciaccatura.

Repeat Bars. The following sign means repeat the previous bar:

This sign placed over the bar line means repeat the two previous bars:

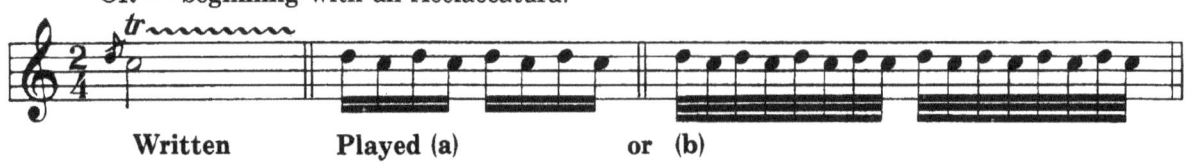

17. THE RUMBLE

COMPLETE THE CHORD TABLE

iv	i	V7
VI	III (+)	ii°
		vii°

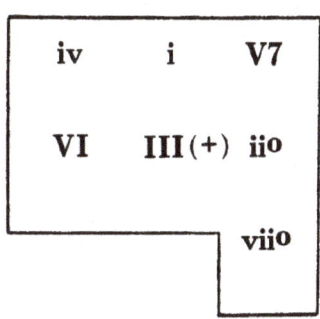

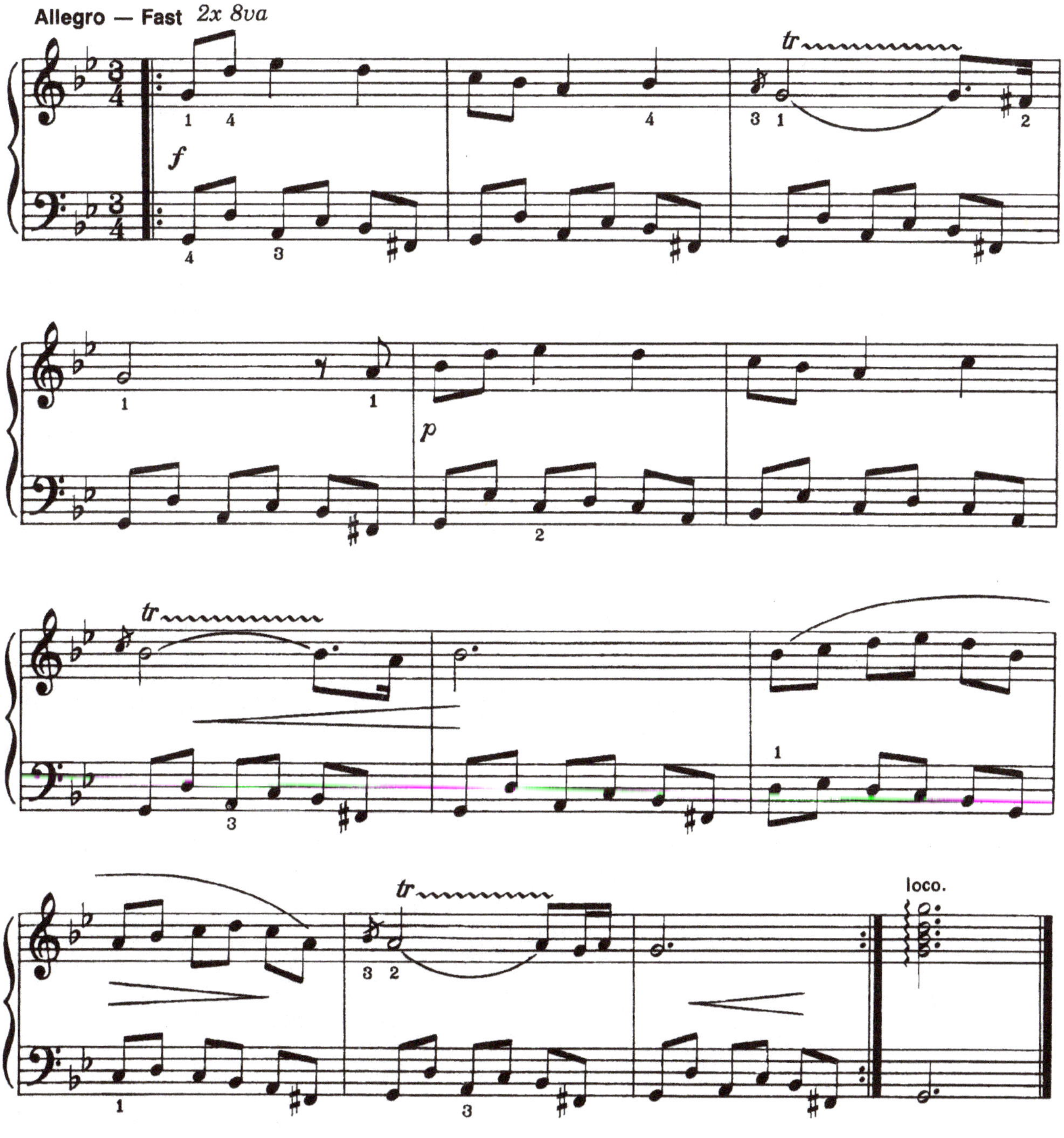

POSITION CHANGING

The main difficulty involved in playing more advanced pieces is the process of moving from one area of the piano to another. Once in the new area, the processes involved in reading and playing, are usually no different to those in easier grade pieces.

There are several things you can do to make moving from one area to another easier. Firstly, work out suitable fingerings to make the connections and secondly, plan your moves in advance. If there is a rest, take full advantage of it to feel the next distance. If there is no rest indicated, but the pedal is used, cut the value of the note short (with the hand only — not the pedal) in order to make your move. It is more important that the next note be played on time than to give the previous note its strict full value.

Use all the fingering devices that you know: finger changes on one note, or on repeated notes, chord or scale fingerings, octave positions, etc, so that you can avoid having to look at your hands and at the keyboard to find the next position.

If all else fails, in other words if the position moves over 2 or 3 octaves in a very short space of time, take a quick glance and make sure you recover your position on the music in as short a time as possible.

NEW POSITION CHANGING METHODS. NUMBER TWO
HELPING HAND INTERVAL READING EXERCISES

Apart from feeling the intervals up to an octave in one hand, these same intervals can be felt from hand to hand.

Place the two hands on ten consecutive notes. Practise playing step (2nd), skip (3rd), skip-plus-one (4th), jump (5th), 6th, 7th and Octave (8th) intervals from hand to hand. For instance, the left hand can begin on the 5th finger and play the intervals up to a 5th and then the right hand can continue to supply the fingers for the intervals of 6th, 7th and Octave. (It could even supply the fingers for the intervals of a 9th and 10th).

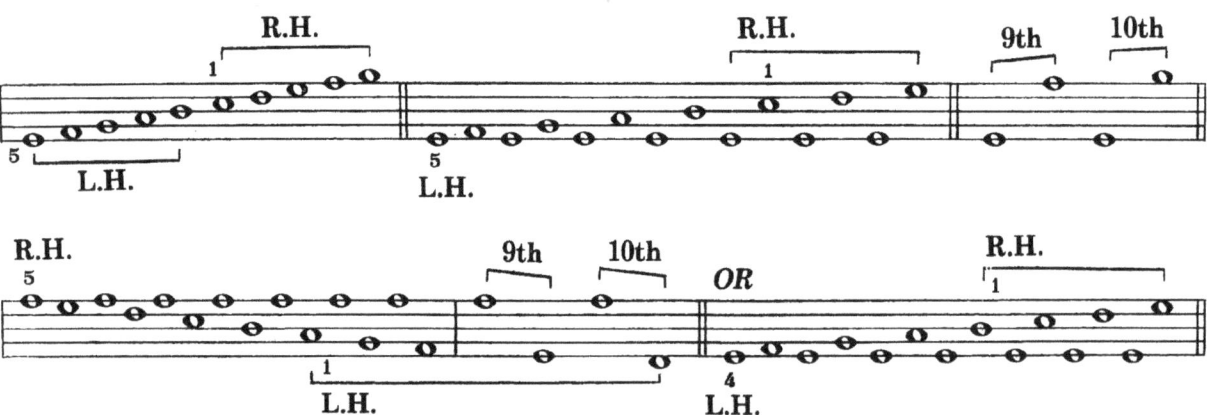

The interval of a sixth could also be felt from the 3rd finger of one hand to the 3rd finger in the next hand if the hands were in close position.

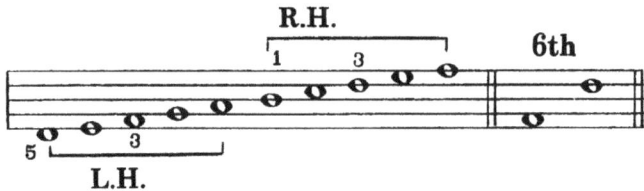

When playing hand-over-hand, the player can judge the next note from the finger that has just been depressed. This can be done in two ways:

(a) by placing the finger of the travelling hand on exactly the same note as has just been played;

(b) by placing the finger of the travelling hand on the note one step away.

From this new position all other intervals can be judged.

Thus:

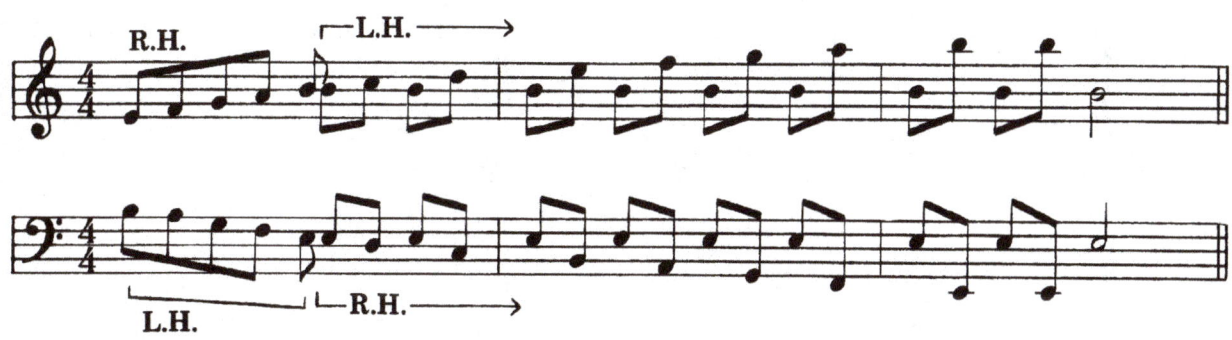

Play the above examples and then move on to the exercises and pieces on the next few pages.

HELPING HAND EXERCISES — Left Hand Crossing Right

Transpose the following exercises to the keys of F, G, D, A, E and B Majors.

18. LEAPING LIZARDS!

HELPING HAND EXERCISES — Right Hand Crossing Left

Transpose to the keys of F, G, D, A, E and B Majors.

19. LEAPING FROGS!

PEDAL POINT or PEDAL BASS
(Also known as ORGAN PEDAL)

Pedal Point is a Harmonic Device which occurs when one note is sustained or repeated (usually in the Bass Part but not always), while a series of different chords are played over it. Usually the series begins on a chord which includes the Pedal Note and finishes the same way.

To be effective, some of the chords in the series should clash with the Pedal Point note and move on to resolve on one of the following chords.

The effect is that of a **DRONE** Bass, similar to that set up by instruments of the Bagpipe family. It is often used in Organ Music as it is easy to put the foot down on one pedal while the hands continue playing the moving lines and chords. Hence the name Organ Pedal.

In sheet music and Jazz Compositions, the Pedal Point will be indicated by being placed under

the chord name thus: $\dfrac{Gmi}{A}$ or sometimes Gmi/A

or sometimes Gmi (A Bass) or $\dfrac{Gmi}{A\ bass}$.

It is only Pedal Point if it continues for at least 2 to 3 chords, thus:

C $\dfrac{Dmi}{C}$ $\dfrac{Emi}{C}$ $\dfrac{F}{C}$ C

Use the same system of placing the chord over the Bass note if you wish to indicate that any note other than the Root Note should be played in the Bass.

$\dfrac{B\flat maj}{A\ bass}$ OR $\dfrac{Cmi}{B\flat}$

When the Pedal note is placed at the top of a series of chords, with the changing harmonies moving underneath it, it is known as a Descant Pedal.

MORE DOMINANT SEVENTH CHORDS

Add to the previous seventh chords (F, C, G, D and A) the Dominant Sevenths on E and B, B flat and E flat. Do not forget to practise the Augmented and Diminished triads learnt previously.

* **Mordent** 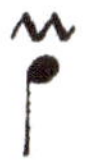

Play the written note, the one above and back to the written note. Once only, quickly.

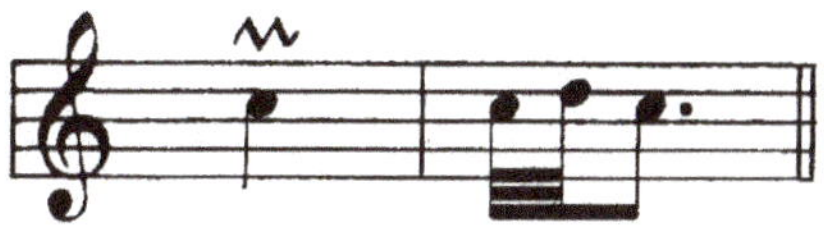

Written Played

20. UNDERCURRENTS

COMPLETE THE CHORD TABLE

IV	I	V7
ii	vi	iii
		vii°

Write the Chord names above the bars (measures).

Presto — Very fast

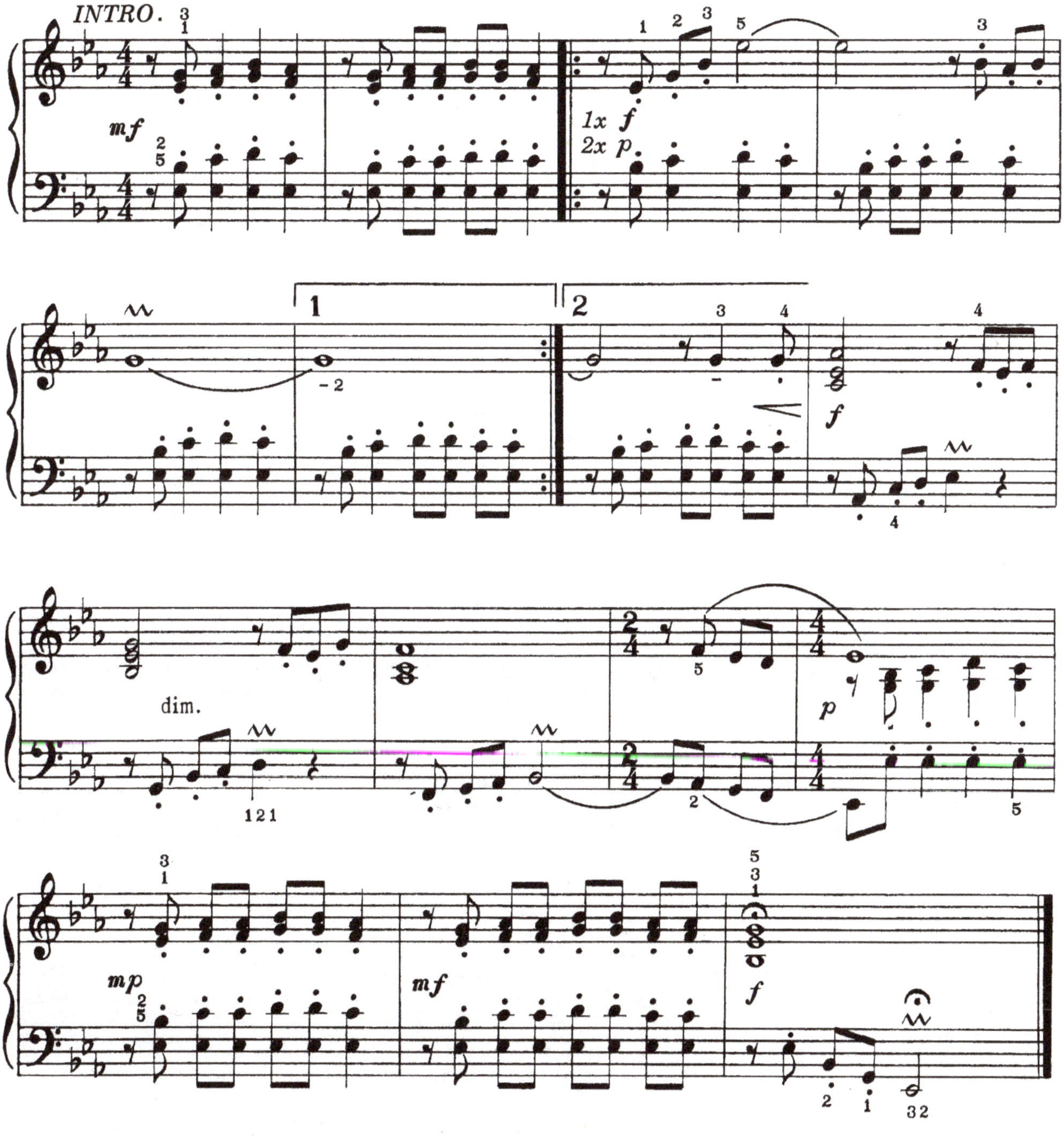

JAZZ TIMING

Many classically trained musicians cannot get the hang of playing music with a swing feel.

The way this feel is achieved is no mystery. The "swing" results when straight quavers are played with a triplet feel, so that they are interpreted thus:

A bar of quavers with this feel may look like this:

or like this: but is interpreted as this:

and counted 1 & a, 2 & a, 3 & a and 4 & a.

So if you see two quavers, place the counting under them so that the first quaver receives "1 &" and the second receives the "a", thus:

1 + a

Following the same idea, a quaver followed by two semi-quavers becomes

1 +   1 + a

Most of the tunes in the "fake" song books (written with only a melody line and chords) which are in 4/4 or C, have this sort of feel unless they are rock tunes. (Rock music is counted the same way as classical music — i.e. straight quavers).

SWING TIMING LISTENING SUGGESTION

Recordings by the Glen Miller Orchestra. For instance, "In the Mood". Recordings by the Tommy Dorsey Orchestra. Piano Music of Art Tatum, Fats Waller, Teddy Wilson, Oscar Peterson, Bill Evans.

Below are several Boogie-Woogie patterns for the Left Hand.
They are all to be interpreted with a "swing" feel.

THE BLUES SCALE

Apart from the Major and Minor scales, thus far mentioned, music from different areas of the world uses many other types of scales. The one we are most used to hearing in the popular music of today is the BLUES SCALE.

The scale has its origin in the African Scales which were carried to America by the Negro slave population.

A **Blues Scale** is formed when the 3rd, 5th and 7th degrees of the major scale are flattened and used instead of the Major scale notes.

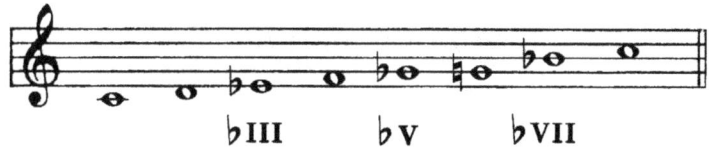

Refer to Contemporary Theory Workbook - Book 2

The Blues Scale therefore has a slightly minor sound to it. However, the Blues Notes (♭3, ♭5, ♭7) gain their effectiveness through being played as part of a Melodic Line at the same time or in close proximity to their equivalent Major Notes in the corresponding chord.

It has been said that we are searching for the Quarter-Tone (half of a semitone) of the African Scales by using the dissonance (clash) created when the Blues note and its matching Major Scale note are played together. As Leonard Bernstein says: "We can produce one on a wind instrument or a stringed instrument or with the voice, but on the piano we have to approximate it by playing together the two notes on each side of it:

The real note is somewhere in there, in that crack between them."

The Joy of Music. Leonard Bernstein. Simon and Schuster. New York. Page 101.

In the Boogie Patterns, given here (page 80), numbers 1 and 3 use the Flattened Fifth degree blues note; number 2 uses the Flattened Third degree (♭3) and number 4 uses the Flattened Seventh (♭7).

Listen for the Blues Notes in Boogie-Woogie and Jazz tunes. When playing your own chord patterns and improvisations use the Blues Notes to add more **Colour** to your playing of the melodic line.

TWELVE - BAR BLUES

Choose a key in which to play the Boogie patterns in a Blues progression. Use the notes of the Blues Scale in your chosen key, to improvise a Right Hand melody over the Left Hand patterns.

CHORD TABLE

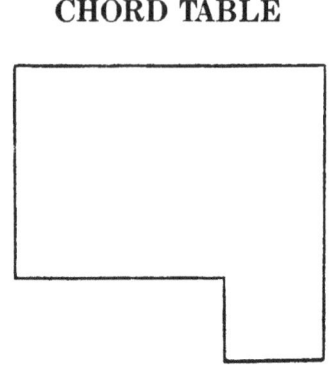

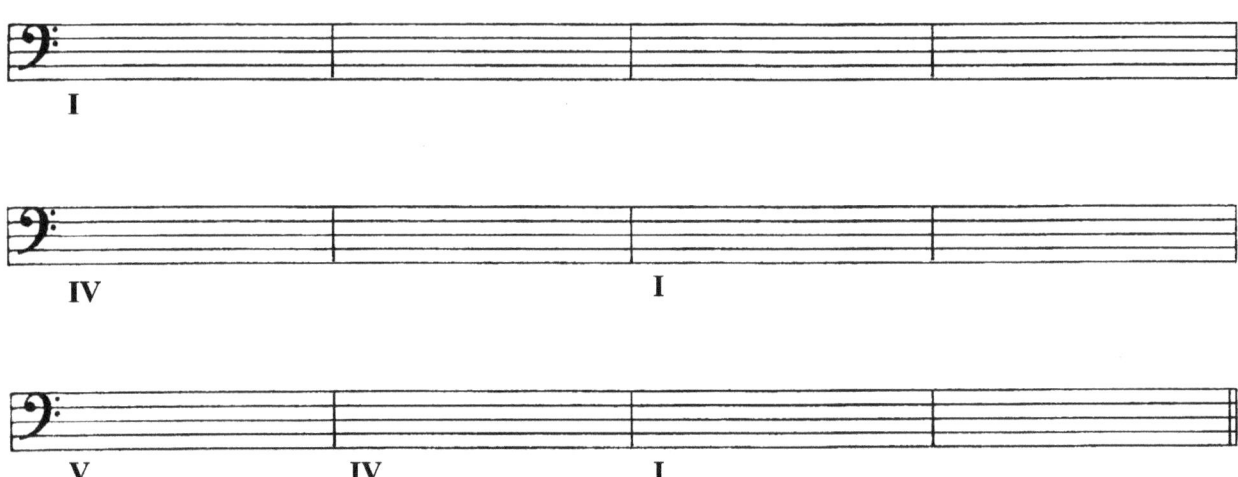

Refer to 'Blues and Boogie-Woogie' (Brandman) for a series of graded pieces to play in this style.
The book includes details on the history of the blues and in depth information on the Blues Progression.

Refer also to the following pieces by Australian composer Kerin Bailey. They are contained in his **Jazzin' Around** series. *Faster Blaster* from Book 5, *Raggy Blues* from Book 2, *Blue Waltz* from Book 3.

F SHARP AND C SHARP HARMONIC MINOR SCALES

F SHARP MINOR

The next set of two minor scales to be learnt are the F sharp and C sharp Minors. F sharp is related to A Major and therefore has three sharps — F, C and G sharps. Play the Natural Minor with the following fingering and then raise the Seventh Degree from E to E sharp (same as the white note F) for the Harmonic Form. The right hand fingering is: 3 4 1 2 3 1 2 3 and the left hand fingering is: 4 3 2 1 3 2 1 3.

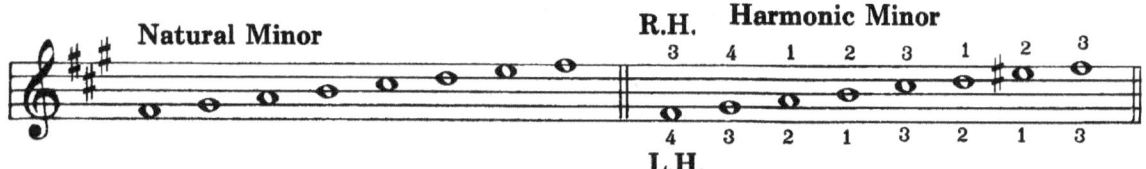

C SHARP MINOR

C sharp minor is related to E Major and therefore has 4 sharps — F, C, G and D sharps. The right hand fingering is exactly the same as for F sharp harmonic Minor, as is the pattern of white, white, black for the 6th, 7th and 8th notes of the two scales. This is why it is useful to think of these two scales as a set. The left hand fingering for C sharp minor is: 3 2 1 4 3 2 1 3. It is in fact the same as for C sharp Major. After you have played C sharp Natural Minor, raise the seventh note from B to B sharp (white note) to convert the scale to the Harmonic Form.

F SHARP AND C SHARP MINOR CHORDS

Two chords derived from these scales are of course F sharp Minor: F sharp, A, C sharp and C sharp Minor: C sharp, E, G sharp. Add these two new chords to the others you have learnt and play them in inversions in block and broken form.

F AND C MINOR CONTRARY MOTION SCALES
Contrary Scales

This lesson you should be ready to learn C and F Harmonic Minors in contrary form. Notice that black notes occur at the same time in C Harmonic Contrary and that all blacks do the same in F Harmonic Contrary except for B flat which falls at the same time as C (white note) in the opposite hand.

DOMINANT SEVENTHS

The last three Dominant Seventh Chords to learn are A flat Seventh, which belongs to the D flat Major scale, D flat Seventh, which belongs to G flat Major scale, and F sharp Seventh, which belongs to B Major scale.

Practise the above chords in both Block and Broken Inversions.

✻ **Inverted Mordent**

As before, only take the lower note.

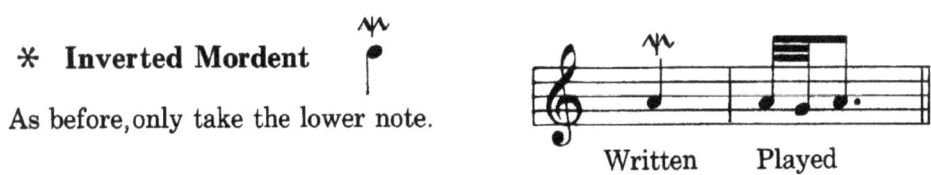

21. GO FOR BAROQUE

Prepare for performance by clapping the rhythm of both parts on your knees.

THE EXTENDED MINOR KEY CHORD TABLE

Keep these chord choices in mind when analysing the first eight bars of this piece. (A)
The B section of this piece includes modulation.
Look ahead to *Contemporary Piano Method Book 2B* for more information.

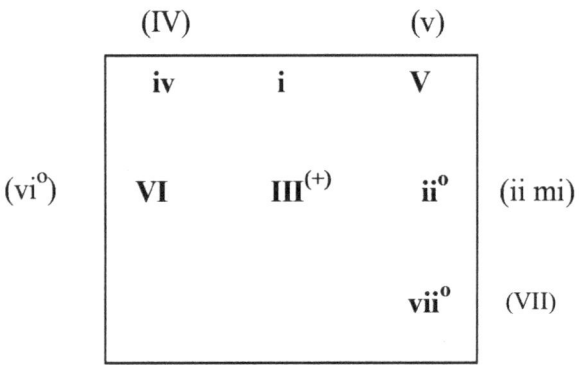

GO FOR BAROQUE

Music Speed-Reading
Tetrad shapes - Root, 1st and 2nd inversions

Here are some more interval exercises with the hand set over the octave span. They are based on the 4-note chord shapes in Root Position, 1st and 2nd inversions, and are fingered accordingly.

Note the extensions between the fingers.

Using the same method as was used previously on the exercises on pages 30 and 46, find the hand-position and set the fingers, then think of each note in relation to its position in the chord shape — as Bottom, Second, Third or Top note of the shape. This way you will be able to read the line of music as one unit, rather than as many separate intervals.

INTERVAL EXERCISES OVER THE OCTAVE SPAN ⌐¬ extension

Root Position Triad Shape

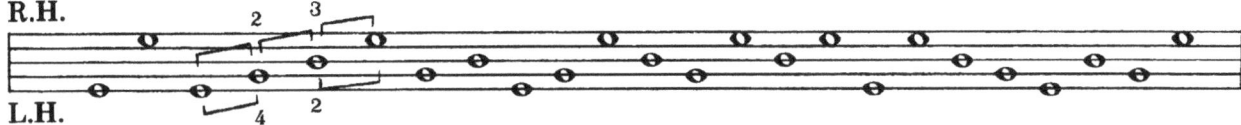

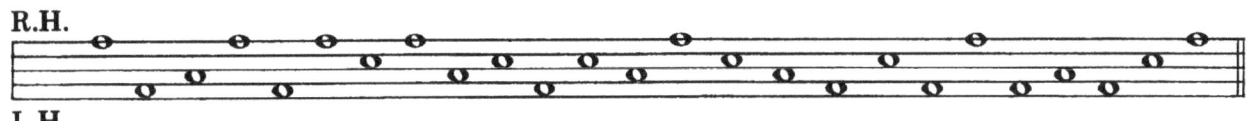

First Inversion Shape

Second Inversion Shape

22. MINUET IN G
First Half

CHORD TABLE

Write the Chord Names above the bars.

JOHANN SEBASTIAN BACH, 1685–1750
German, Baroque

CHORD PROGRESSIONS

Here are two chord progressions moving around the Cycle of Fifths. They use triads that we have already learnt, Major and Minor, and the Dominant seventh of the key as the second last chord. Try to transpose them to all twelve major keys and play them in both the given forms. [(a) and (b)].

Notice how closely placed the notes are from one chord to the next (voice leading) and try to do the same in your other transpositions. Try starting each progression on a different inversion of the Tonic Triad. You will find the chords if you work out the chord tables for each key you wish to play in.

CHORD TABLE

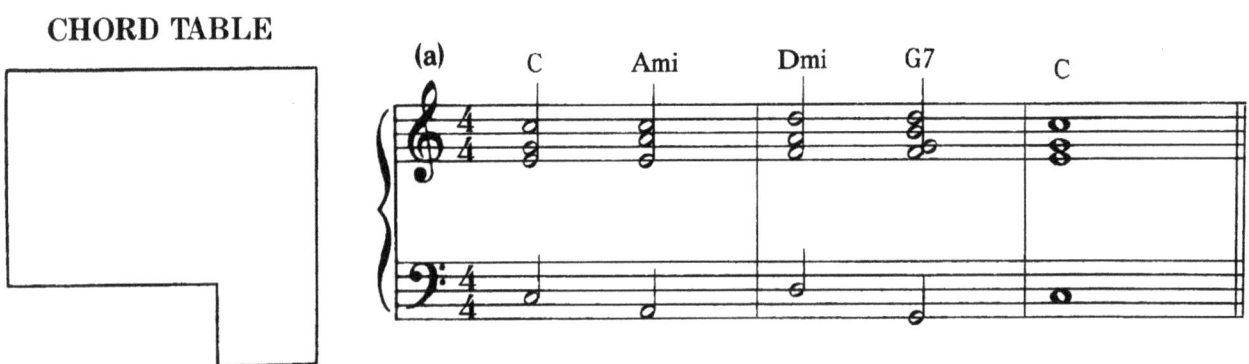

Write the degree numbers of the Root Notes of this progression.

. . . .

CHORD TABLE

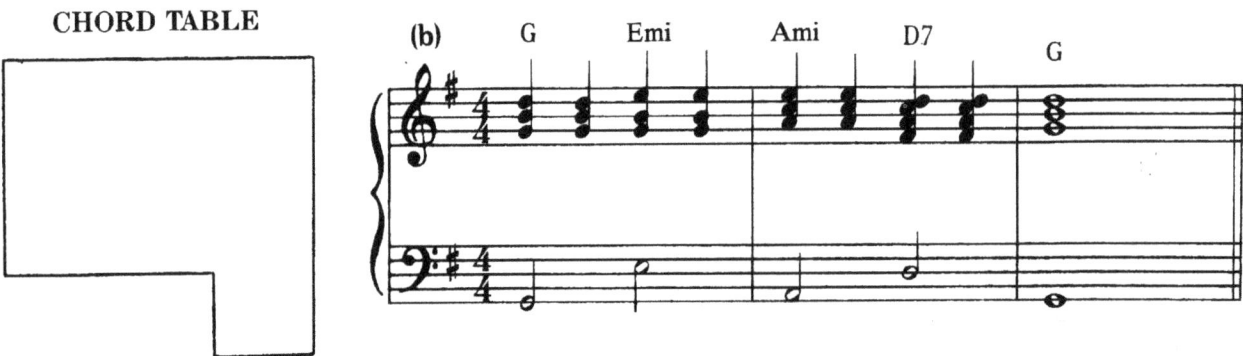

IMPROVISING ON A CHORD PATTERN

In Book 1, a system of improvising was introduced on page 102. This system can once again be used with the addition of the new chords that have been learned in this second book.

Play one chord per bar in the Left Hand; either as one long chord or sounding it again on each beat of the bar.

Next, choose one note from the chord as a melody note for the Right Hand and move from it to the other notes of the chord, using the scale notes as passing notes. If all the chords belong to the one Chord Table you can use the Tonic scale notes as passing notes for all the chords.

For instance, if the passage is in G scale and uses the chords of the G table, play the notes of chord vi, E minor chord (E, G, B) and link them up with notes from the G scale. In this case, F sharp and A. Likewise, if you are using the notes of chord IV, C chord (C, E, G) you can use D and F sharp as passing notes.

Try an improvised line in 4/4 and in 3/4 time signatures. Start with half notes (minims ♩) and quarter notes (crotchets ♩) and then gradually add eighth notes (quavers ♪) and dotted notes (♩. or ♩. ♪). Remember also to use **rests,** accents and staccato notes to make the melody more interesting.

Here are some suggested rhythms for 4/4:

Here are some suggested rhythms for 3/4:

Improvising Practice

Once you have worked out the chords for a tune, you can write them out as a chord pattern to use as a basis for improvisation. Alternatively, you can improvise straight form the chords written above each bar for the tune. Improvise your own melody to the chord progression for *'Sans Souci Shuffle'* on pages 92 and 93.

Another suggestions is play both an improvised line and the melody line as a duet with a friend. Ask the friend to play the melody line on either another instrument or at the upper end of the piano. Play an improvised line with the right hand while supplying the chords in the left hand. Listen for notes which clash with the melody note and resolve the dissonant notes to a note either side. If the written melody has long notes, your improvised line can employ faster moving notes. Conversely if the written melody is quite busy, then play longer value notes in your improvised line.

Music Speed Reading
New position changing Methods 3
Shifting shapes over the interval of the third

The following exercises involve a change of hand position over the distance of a skip or third.
The way to feel the position change is to skim the fingers lightly over the cracks between the keys until you have the confidence to judge the distance comfortably.

If the intervals or chord positions being played are the same each time, you need only read the distances between the lowest note of each chord or 6th interval. The distances in each of these exercises are only steps or skips.

Start each exercise on any white note you wish. Use the first and fifth fingers for each interval of a sixth and the correct triad fingering for each hand for the chord exercises.

Once you have found the position, keep the fingers set over the interval distance and simply move the hand as one unit.

The Shuffle Rhythm

The shuffle rhythm was a popular 'feel' for many Rock tunes of the 1950s. The rhythm is written as dotted eighth note followed by a sixteenth,

but is interpreted with a triplet feel similar to the Boogie-Woogie patterns shown on page 80.

The Shuffle rhythm itself is a development from the Boogie-Woogie rhythm which emerged in the Southern American states in the 1920s and was also used in many Swing Jazz tunes of the 1930s and 1940s.

Some of the well-known songs which use this rhythm are: * *Shake, Rattle and Roll,* * *Bad, Bad Leroy Brown,* * *Chattanooga Choo-Choo* and * *Guitar Boogie Shuffle.*

Below are some two-handed styles in which to play a Shuffle Rhythm accompaniment. A style of accompaniment for Left Hand only, is demonstrated on the following pages in *Sans Souci Shuffle*.

SHUFFLE RHYTHM PATTERNS FOR TWO HANDS

Practise these shuffle rhythm patterns in all twelve Major Keys.

23. SANS SOUCI SHUFFLE

This piece changes key in the B section to E minor. Therefore you will need to complete two chord tables to be able to analyse the chord progression. Mark any I vi ii V I progressions with a bracket.

A SECTION CHORD TABLE

B SECTION CHORD TABLE

CADENCES

A Cadence is a musical ending formula consisting of two chords.

There are four types of cadences in common use.

1) The Authentic Cadence also known as the Perfect Cadence or Full Close
2) The Plagal Cadence
3) The Semicadence or Half Cadence also known as an Imperfect Cadence
4) The Interrupted Cadence also known as the Deceptive Cadence or Surprise Cadence

The Full Close. Budding pianists who have been completing the 'Chord Tables' for each piece and naming the chords in each bar as they have been working through this series, will by now have observed that in many pieces the Dominant Chord (V) occurs as the second last chord and is most frequently followed by the final Tonic Chord.

This movement **V - I (Major Key); V - i (minor key)** is labelled an Authentic Cadence (USA) and Perfect Cadence (UK). Sometimes chord vii (a diminished chord) is used as a substitute for chord V as the two chords share two common notes.

The Plagal Cadence. A less strong finish can be established by the use of this cadence, which is often known as the 'Amen' cadence. Listen to the falling effect as you play this progression. The chord movement is **IV - I (Major Key); iv - i (minor key)**.

Both the above cadences can be used as *final* cadences bringing the chord movement to rest on the Tonic Chord. The next two cadences are used only to end phrases in the body of the piece. They are known as *intermediary* cadences.

The Half Close. The Semicadence (USA), Imperfect Cadence (UK) has the opposite function to a Full Close. The chord movement in each of the four versions of the Half Close ends on the Dominant chord (V).
   a) I – V (Major Key); i – V (minor key)
   b) ii – V (Major Key); ii° – V (minor key)
   c) IV – V (Major Key); iv – V (minor key)
   d) vi – V (Major Key); VI – V (minor key)

The Interrupted, Deceptive or **Surprise Cadence**. The chord movement is from Dominant to Submediant **(V – vi)) (V - VI)**. In a <u>major</u> key, chord **vi** is the *relative minor chord* (surprise!) and in a <u>minor</u> key chord **VI** is a *Major chord* (surprise!).

Play all the cadences on the following pages to hear the effect of the chord movements. Notice how the Authentic and Plagal cadences create the feeling of finality and how the intermediary cadences set up an expectation for a balancing phrase to complete the musical sentence.

To learn to write four-part harmony and cadences plus discover more interesting information on the topic, refer to **Harmony Comes Together** *(MMP8081) Brandman.*
Cadence information is included on pages 76-90 of HCT.

CADENCES

Play and listen to the following cadences and progressions.
Transpose them to all twelve Major Keys and to all the minor keys you have learnt.

PERFECT CADENCES

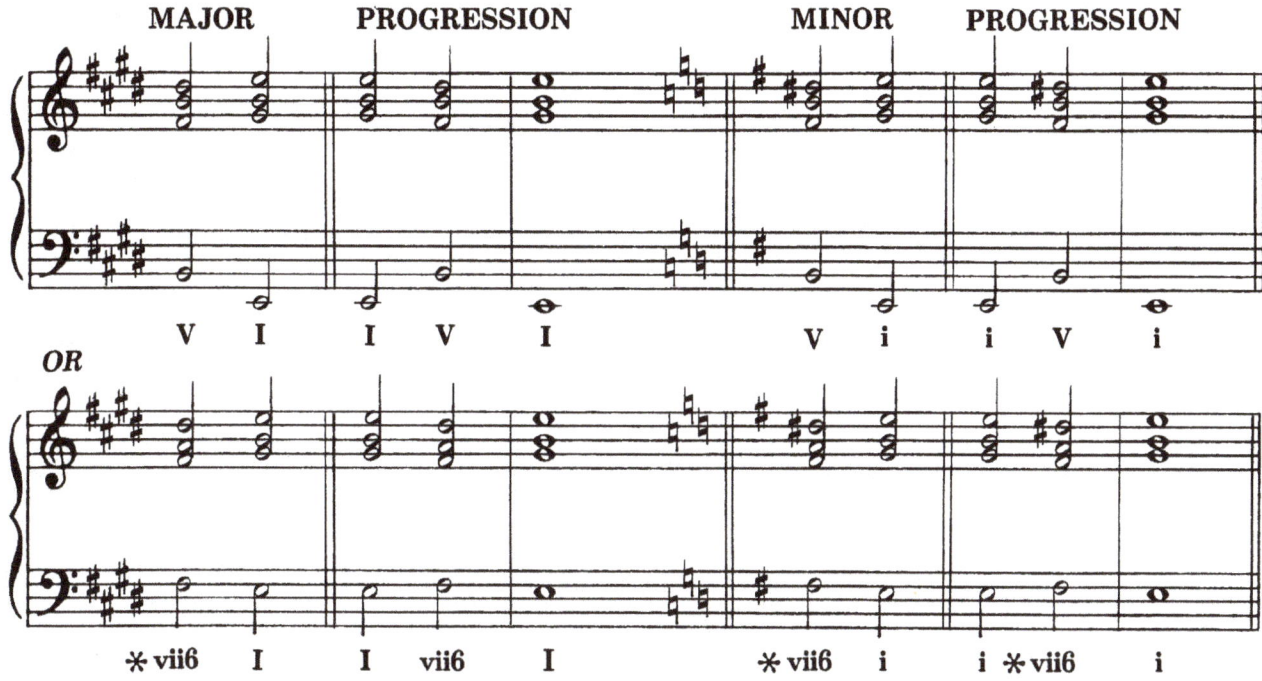

✲ Usually used in 1st Inversion

PLAGAL CADENCES

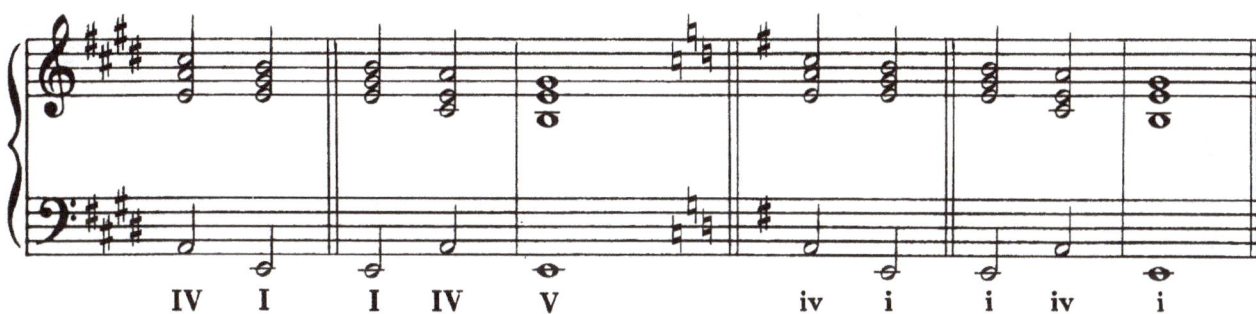

The above Cadences are written in PIANO STYLE, that is, with one note in the Bass Clef and three notes in the Treble Clef in close position.

They could also be written in VOCAL STYLE. In Vocal Style each of the four notes in the chord represents one of the four voices: Bass (low male voice), Tenor (high male voice), Alto (short for Contralto — low female voice) and Soprano (high female voice). The stems are drawn up for the Soprano and Tenor parts and down for the Alto and Bass parts.

Provided that the parts are not too widely spaced, most Cadences or Four-Part Harmony arrangements are still playable on the keyboard.

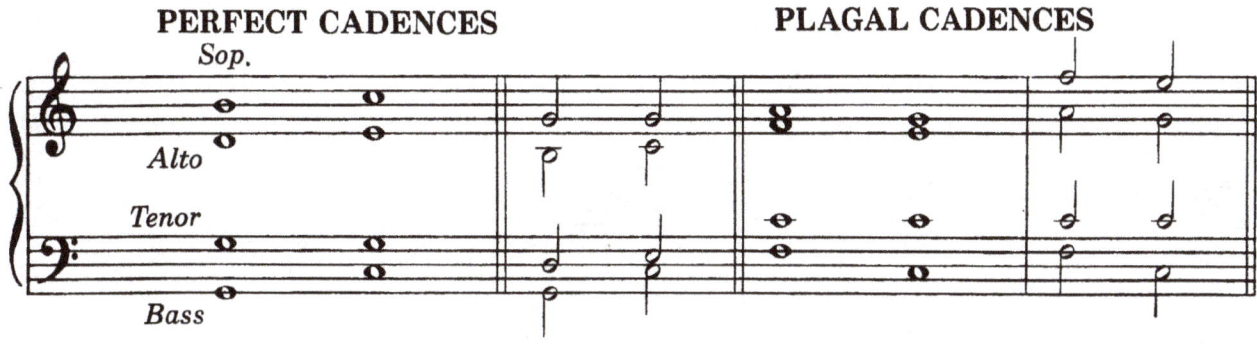

IMPERFECT CADENCES

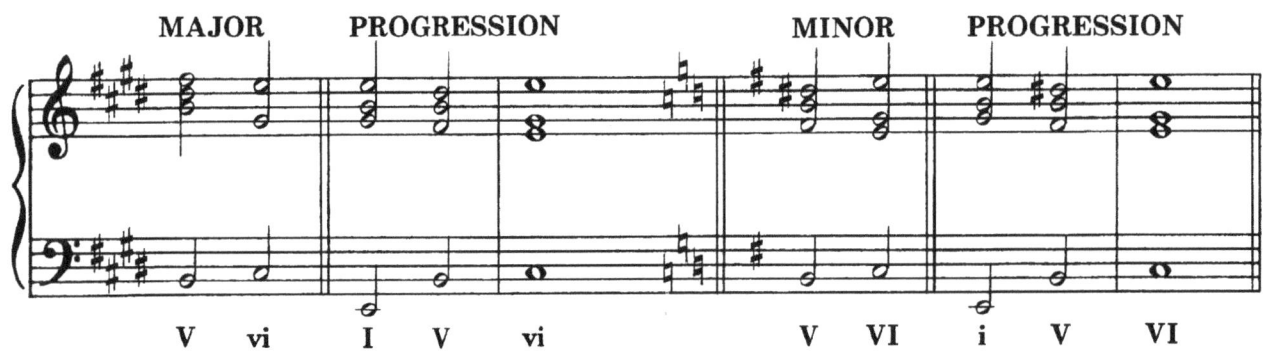

INTERRUPTED CADENCES

Tremolo or Shake Play each note alternating, several times quickly. Written Played

24. BOOGIE SHAKE

CHORD TABLE

Write the names of the chords found on the first beat of each bar.

SWING FEEL

Moderato

DIMINISHED 7TH CHORDS

This type of chord is very important and interesting to know. We have already seen (on page 38) how to build and find Diminished Triads. (Each note is three semitones from the next). If we add a diminished seventh "interval" to the triad, the resulting chord is a Diminished Seventh Chord. (See example a). Each note is "equidistant" from the next. That is: there are 3 semitones between all four of the notes. (Five if you want to add the octave.)

Because of this fact, and the fact that there are 12 semitones in the octave, you will find that there are only three diminished seventh chord shapes. They can be written 12 different ways but you will find that the notes on the keyboard always fit into one of the three shapes.

Build Diminished Seventh on C, C sharp and D. When you play them in their inversions you will see the Cdim7th is the same as E flat, F sharp and Adim7ths; C sharp dim 7th is the same as E, G and B flat dim7ths; and Ddim7th is the same as F, A flat and Bdim7ths. (See example b).

In sheet music the Circle for Diminished (o) usually means play a Diminished 7th chord. You will have to use your taste and Harmonic knowledge to judge if only a diminished triad is needed in some cases.

Another point of interest is the fact that due to one dim7th being the same as three others, they can be very handy "pivot" chords to take the music from one key to another.

As I pointed out in page 38, the diminished triad is found on the seventh degree and has a leading function back to the tonic of the key. The Dim7th has the same effect. Thus Bdim7 leads back to C Major (or Minor). However, if you realise that Bdim7 is the same as Ddim7 then it could also lead back to E flat Major (or Minor) (vii-Ddim to VIII-E flat).

Likewise, the same chord is also Fdim7, leading to G flat Major, and G sharp dim7 leading to A Major. (See example c.)

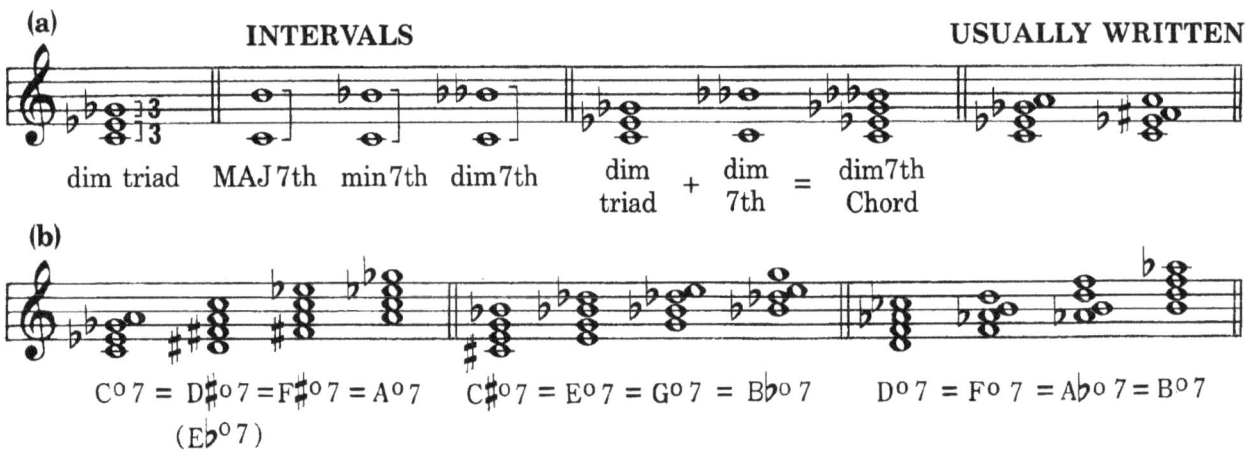

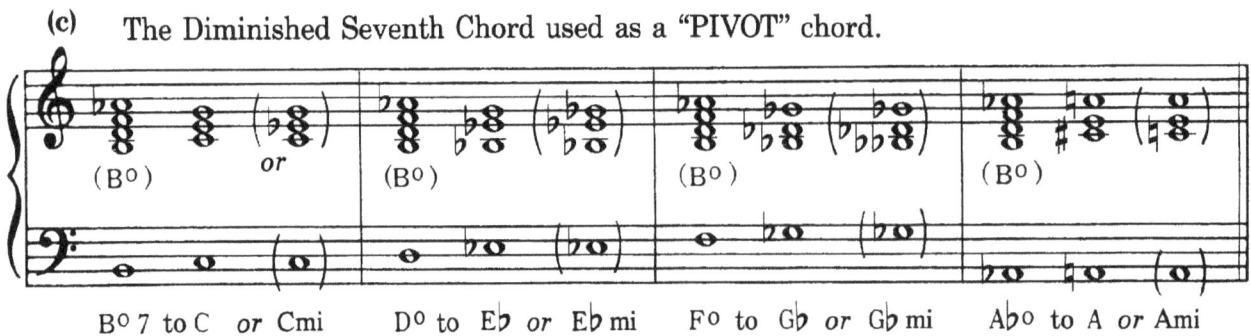

(c) The Diminished Seventh Chord used as a "PIVOT" chord.

*Refer to **Pictorial Patterns for Keyboard Scales and Chords** for practice suggestions on the resolution of Diminished 7th chords.*

CHORD PATTERN

Here is an example of a chord pattern using the chords studied thus far. It is in 3/4 time and is typical of an accompaniment pattern to a waltz tune.

It is based on the cycle of fifths but uses a Dim 7th on the seventh degree as the penultimate (second to last) chord, instead of the dominant seventh chord.

1. Play the example as written.
2. Play the chords in the left hand and improvise a melody line with the right hand.
3. Name the Cadence marked: ⌐⎯⎯⎯¬
4. Transpose the example and play it in several different keys.

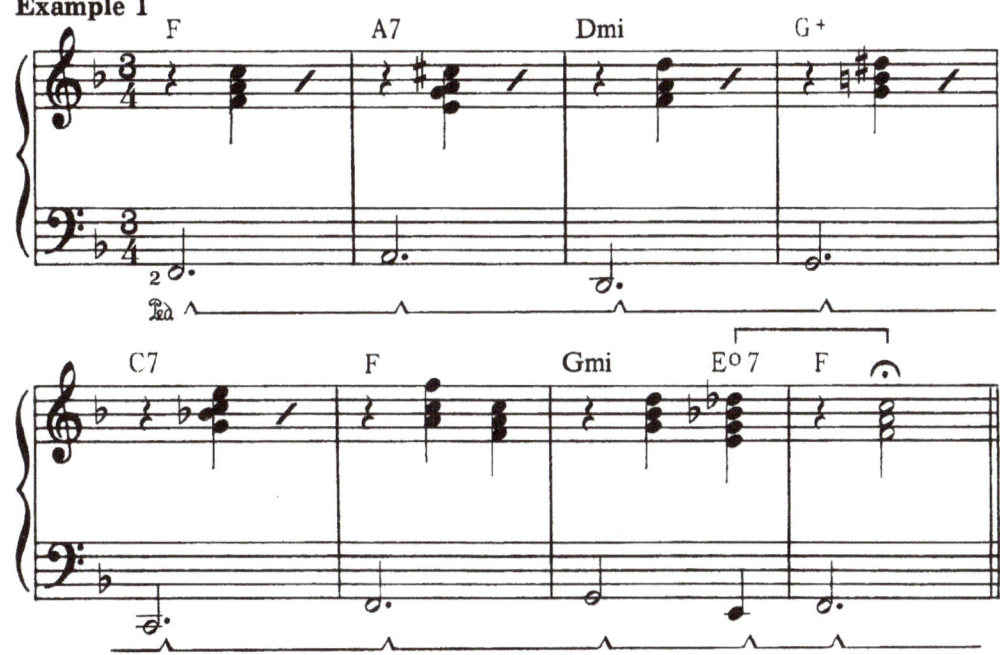

Example 2 employs an alternative style of accompaniment based on the same chord pattern as example 1. The Left Hand pattern uses the notes of the chords in Broken form.

Similar flowing patterns can be devised to suit many different tunes. Keep this style in mind when you are required to provide an accompaniment, based on a chord pattern, or when you are required to supply the Left Hand part to a single melody line in a song from a "Fake" book.

TURN

Take the **Keynote,** the note **above, Keynote,** the note **below** and return to the **Keynote. N.B.** The upper and lower notes must be taken from the scale unless otherwise indicated.

25. ON THE UPTURN

CHORD TABLE

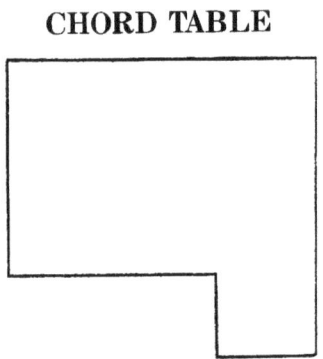

Name the Chords in each bar.

Name the Cadences marked. ⌐‾‾‾¬

1. ....
2. ....

ON THE UPTURN

MAJOR SCALE GRAND PICTORIAL PATTERN OVERVIEW

Here is a **Grand Pictorial Pattern** of the Major Scale pathways and their Key Signatures.

Read each column from top to bottom and notice how the patterns 'grow' as each one adds another sharp or flat. Observe how the positions of the black notes remain the same, as an extra black note is added to each scale.

Enharmonic Scales.

The scale pathway for D Flat Major is the same as for C Sharp Major, only the white notes are named differently. The same applies to F Sharp and G Flat major scales.

Relate the scales presented on this page to the Cycle of Fifths on page 14.

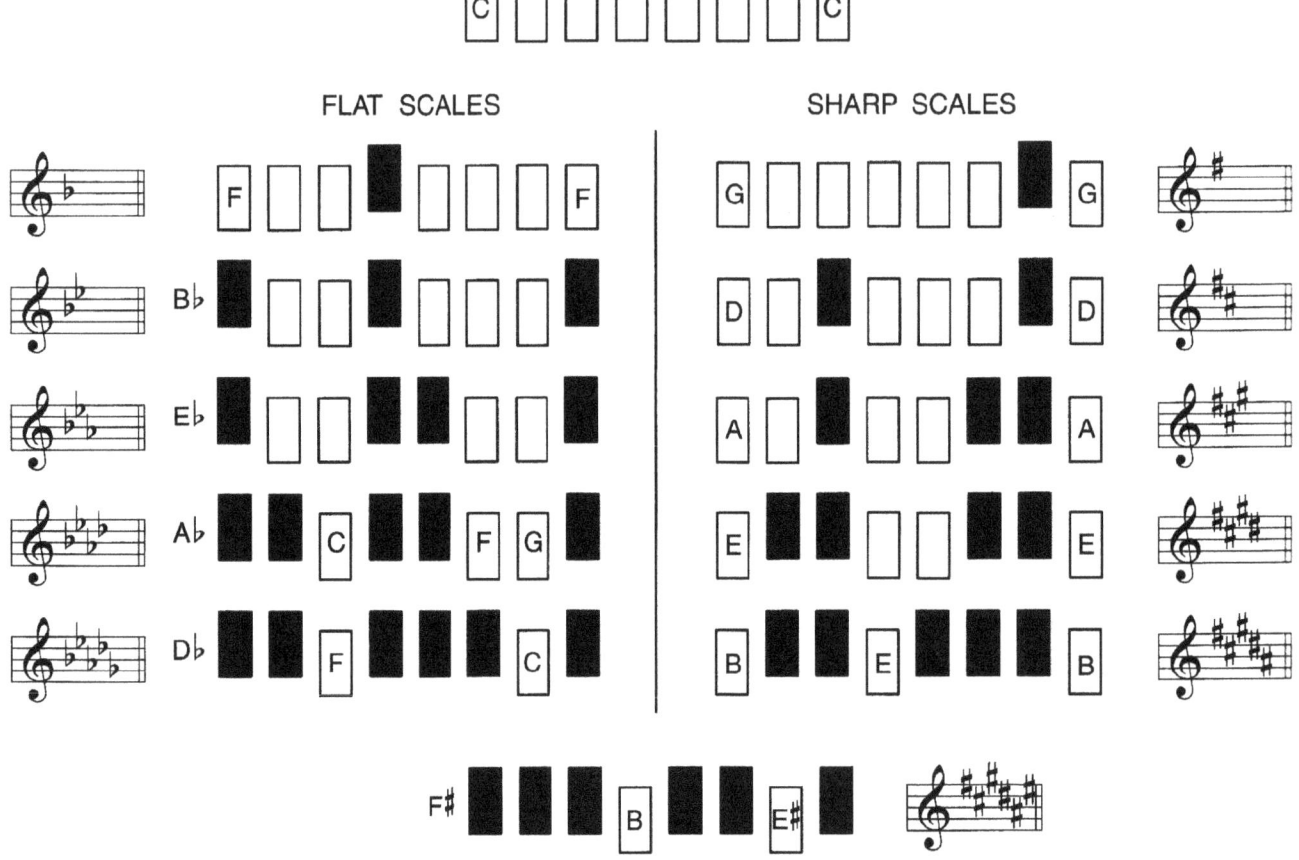

SUMMARY OF SCALE FINGERING

		Left Hand	Right Hand
Group 1:	C G D A E	5 4 3 2 1 3 2 1	1 2 3 1 2 3 4 5
Group 2:	B	4 3 2 1 4 3 2 1	Same as Group 1
	F	Same as Group 1	1 2 3 4 1 2 3 4
Group 3:	B flat	3 2 1 4 3 2 1 3	4 1 2 3 1 2 3 4
	E flat	" " " " " " "	3 1 2 3 4 1 2 3
	A flat	" " " " " " "	3 4 1 2 3 1 2 3
	D flat	" " " " " " "	2 3 1 2 3 4 1 2
Group 4:	F sharp	4 3 2 1 3 2 1 3	2 3 4 1 2 3 1 2

N.B. 4 falls on B♭ (A♯) in RH.

MARGARET BRANDMAN'S INTEGRATED SUPPORT MATERIALS FOR THIS LEVEL

TECHNICAL

* Pictorial Patterns for Keyboard Scales and Chords - *graphic patterns to help students learn the keyboard pathways for scales, along with helpful hints on fingering, plus a comprehensive practise planner for daily scale and chord practice.*

IMPROVISATION SKILLS

* It's Easy to Improvise - *information on how to add left hand accompaniments to single melody lines with chord symbols, and improvise or embellish a Right Hand line. Introducing many chord types applied to many gently graded well-known melodies and. Providing more practice in the accompaniment skills employed on pages 42 and 43 of this book.*

REPERTOIRE

* Dreamweaving – *Five concert pieces exploring modern chords and modal relationships. Each tuneful piece is composed with a varied set of technical challenges and features a different four-note chord (e.g. Major 7th) along with linked scales or modes.*

* Twelve Timely Pieces – *Tuneful performance pieces in varying time signatures from 2/4 to 7/4, progressing gradually through major and minor key signatures up to two sharps and flats.*

* Contemporary Modal Pieces - *a graded set of contemporary modal pieces featuring unusual rhythms and interesting harmonies. Each with an Australian animal title.*

* The Blues and Boogie-Woogie - *12 original Blues and Boogie pieces in major and minor keys, demonstrating various ways of writing the swing feel, and exploring many Left Hand boogie patterns.*

AURAL
* Contemporary Aural Course – Sets 2 to 6
* Contemporary Aural Course - Set 7 - Hear Your Chords!
* Contemporary Aural Course - Set 8 - Hear More Chords!

THEORY/CHORD UNDERSTANDING/HARMONY
* Contemporary Theory Workbooks 1 and 2
* Contemporary Chord Workbook -Book 1
* Harmony Comes Together

RHYTHM
Suggested complementary books:
* Modern Reading Text in 4/4 by Louis Bellson and Gil Breines (Adler Publications)
* Rhythm Unravelled Book and CD by Australian author - Kerin Bailey

HANDY MANUSCRIPT PAGE

www.ingramcontent.com/pod-product-compliance
Lightning Source LLC
Chambersburg PA
CBHW081351160426
43198CB00015B/2586